"When we find ourselves coping with pain, the kitchen can become our therapist, food our source of comfort. The joy of cooking was certainly the salve that soothed the emotional wounds that the journalist Paula Butturini endured. . . . [A] blunt and brave memoir . . . *Keeping the Feast* shares with Julie Powell's *Julie and Julia* and Elizabeth Gilbert's *Eat, Pray, Love* the insight that food can jump-start a journey toward solace." —*The New York Times Book Review*

"Life doesn't always turn out quite the way we had planned. Foreign correspondents Paula Butturini and John Tagliabue were living a charmed existence, falling in love in Rome in 1985, marrying four years later. And then their world collapsed. Butturini's touching memoir proves that daily routines can be comforting and that mealtime should always be a celebration." —*USA Today*

"Brings tears to the eyes." —*San Francisco Chronicle*

"In this moving account . . . Butturini describes how she turned to the familiar comforts of preparing meals to maintain control as her husband spiraled into darkness . . . *Feast* is a reminder that food sustains not only bodies but souls as well." —*People* (3½ stars)

"Most books about food focus on the taste of it—the flavors, textures, and aromas. *Keeping the Feast* acknowledges another important dimension of food—the pleasure of sharing it with someone you love, even when that someone is struggling. [Butturini's] enthusiasm, for food as well as for life, comes across powerfully in her writing." —*St. Petersburg Times*

"If food is love and love heals, does that mean food heals? Paula Butturini proves the equation in gorgeous yet unadorned prose. I will never, ever forget this book."

—Patricia Volk, author of *Stuffed* and *To My Dearest Friends*

"Written with grace and courage, Paula Butturini's *Keeping the Feast* is about the endurance of love in the face of overwhelming odds—depression, tragedy, loss. But it is also about the comfort to be found in the dailiness of life, when every humble act becomes an act of faith; when the preparation and sharing of three good meals a day, however simple, is both a reminder and a celebration—an insistence on celebration—of what life offers. *Keeping the Feast* is a triumph of will and spirit. It made me hungry for everything."

—Abigail Thomas, author of *A Three Dog Life*

"It is a celebration of the human spirit, persevering in the face of overwhelming obstacles, and a paean to the restorative ability of food to bring comfort and peace to our souls as well as our bodies."   —*BookPage*

"Paula Butturini writes magnificently of the pleasures of eating and of how food can be a rare refuge from suffering. Joy and sorrow both have their place on the plate of our lives, and Butturini's experiences have allowed her a unique appreciation of how time around the table with those for whom we care deeply can put us back together. A transcendent memoir."

—Giulia Melucci, author of *I Loved, I Lost, I Made Spaghetti*

"*Keeping the Feast* is a remarkable story, gorgeously told. We reflect, relish, grieve, and heal our way with Paula Butturini, who is wise about so many things—family and place; depression, religion, and love; the disastrous long-term fallout of a single bullet fired at a loved one; and the immediate restorative pleasures of a single Italian meal. This book evokes life at its most serious and dire, and at its most mysterious and delectable. Read it, and be deepened and refreshed."

—Krista Tippett, host of the public radio program
and the book *Speaking of Faith*

Joan,
One of the best things about moving back has been getting to know people for the first time outside of the walls of Cathedral even if it is nearly 50 years late!
Paula

Keeping the Feast

One Couple's Story of Love, Food, and Healing

P A U L A   B U T T U R I N I

RIVERHEAD BOOKS
New York

RIVERHEAD BOOKS
Published by the Penguin Group
Penguin Group (USA) Inc.
375 Hudson Street, New York, New York 10014, USA
Penguin Group (Canada), 90 Eglinton Avenue East, Suite 700, Toronto, Ontario M4P 2Y3, Canada
(a division of Pearson Penguin Canada Inc.)
Penguin Books Ltd., 80 Strand, London WC2R 0RL, England
Penguin Group Ireland, 25 St. Stephen's Green, Dublin 2, Ireland (a division of Penguin Books Ltd.)
Penguin Group (Australia), 250 Camberwell Road, Camberwell, Victoria 3124, Australia
(a division of Pearson Australia Group Pty. Ltd.)
Penguin Books India Pvt. Ltd., 11 Community Centre, Panchsheel Park, New Delhi—110 017, India
Penguin Group (NZ), 67 Apollo Drive, Rosedale, North Shore 0632, New Zealand
(a division of Pearson New Zealand Ltd.)
Penguin Books (South Africa) (Pty.) Ltd., 24 Sturdee Avenue, Rosebank, Johannesburg 2196,
South Africa

Penguin Books Ltd., Registered Offices: 80 Strand, London WC2R 0RL, England

The publisher does not have any control over and does not assume any responsibility for author or third-party websites or their content.

Copyright © 2010 by Paula Butturini
Book design by Jessica Shatan Heslin / Studio Shatan, Inc.

"A Pure Desire on a Gloomy Drab Day" is used by permission of the Estate of John Tagliabue.

First Riverhead hardcover edition: February 2010
First Riverhead trade paperback edition: February 2011
Riverhead trade paperback ISBN: 978-1-59448-500-8

The Library of Congress has catalogued the Riverhead hardcover edition as follows:

Butturini, Paula.

    Keeping the feast: one couple's story of love, food, and healing in Italy / Paula Butturini.
        p.   cm.
    ISBN 978-1-59448-897-9
1. Butturini, Paula.   2. Butturini, Paula—Marriage.   3. Married people—United States—
Biography.   4. Married people—Italy—Biography.   5. Italy—Social life and customs.   6. Cookery—
Italy—Psychological aspects.   7. Victims of violent crimes—Romania—Biography.   8. Gunshot
wounds—Case studies.   9. Wound healing—Italy—Case studies.   10. Mental healing—Italy—Case
studies.   I. Title.
CT275.B83795A3   2010   2009036224
945.091092′2—dc22

PRINTED IN THE UNITED STATES OF AMERICA

10   9   8   7   6   5   4   3   2   1

Penguin is committed to publishing works of quality and integrity.
In that spirit, we are proud to offer this book to our readers; however,
the story, the experiences, and the words are the author's alone.

For Julia, Anna, and Peter,
and, of course, for John

Therefore let us keep the feast,

not with old leaven,

nor the leaven of malice and wickedness,

but with the unleavened bread of sincerity and truth.

—1 Corinthians 5:8

Keeping the Feast

Prologue

*T*wo ghosts. That was how a friend later described us when we returned to Rome in 1992. John and I had been away five years, and though neither of us knew it at the time, we returned, I think, because Rome seemed the most likely place to recuperate and cast out the demons we had picked up in our absence.

We moved into a small apartment near the Tiber on one of those golden October days so perfect that you could never imagine willingly leaving the city again. Every morning I would walk down our narrow street toward the hubbub of Campo dei Fiori, where the flower sellers, the fruit vendors, the vegetable sellers, the fishmongers, the mushroom lady, the bread shop, the lamb and chicken lady, the pork butcher, the notions man, the meat vans, the olive and herb vendors, the newspaper kiosk, the housewares stand, and the roving garlic salesmen from Bangladesh were always open for business no matter how early I awakened.

Morning after morning for an entire year, I walked to the Campo before most people were up. Noisy, honking, shouting Rome is almost quiet at that hour, and what began as a simple routine soon took on the trappings of ritual. I woke up early, dressed, walked out the door and over to the Campo. I would buy a shiny, plump purple-black eggplant. Or a handful of slender green beans, so fresh and young you could eat them raw. I bought three golden pears, or a heavy bunch of fat, green grapes. I bought a few slices of Milanese salami, a bit of veal. I bought a thin slab of creamy Gorgonzola, to spread on crusty, still-warm bread. I bought milk, yogurt, butter, and eggs, and finally the newspapers. Then I would head home, stopping in the tiny church of Santa Brigida, which lay halfway between the Campo and our apartment. The first few months, I would rest my bundles on the cold marble floor, kneel for a moment at the back of the church under the gaze of a painted Madonna, and try not to cry. Months later, I would still kneel for a moment in the same spot, but when I felt the tears coming, I'd make a fist and pound once or twice on the pew in front of me. It made a fitting, hollow sound in the almost empty church. Then I would collect my bundles and continue my short walk home.

I needed both parts of the ritual, the buying of the food and the stopping in the church. We all must eat, and there is nothing more normal than buying the food that keeps us alive. When I performed the ritual of buying our daily bread, the world seemed more normal. Pounding a pew a few minutes later brought home how far from normal I still felt.

Though the name means "Field of Flowers," Campo dei Fiori has not been a meadow since Pope Eugene IV ordered the field scythed and cobblestoned in the 1430s. These days the only flowers are the cut variety on sale at one end of the square and a few pots of scraggly geraniums and shrubs outlining the sidewalk cafés and trattorie and pizza joints that ring the piazza. Since the fifteenth century the Campo has been a horse market, a way station for pilgrims who thronged its Renaissance hostelries, and a place of torture and execution for those branded heretics by the Holy Roman Inquisition. Only since 1869, after the popes' temporal powers had finally been checked, has it been transformed into a public marketplace.

Today money changes hands under a patchwork canvas ceiling of gigantic umbrellas and tarps that protect the produce from Rome's fierce sun. The flower sellers jam their lilies, mums, dahlias, daisies, freesia, eucalyptus, sweet williams, and roses into plastic buckets and vases, enough to form a wall of flowers toward the western end of the square. All the other vendors display their wares willy-nilly, piled high in bursts of brilliant colors atop weather-beaten wooden carts or sawhorse tables. When business is slow, and often when it's not, the vendors converse in deep-toned shouts with their competitors or the crowd.

From shortly after dawn till shortly after lunchtime, unruly knots of shoppers (I doubt the Campo has ever seen an orderly line, even for a hanging or a burning at the stake) jostle for position around the stands to choose the makings for their next meal. By one-thirty p.m. business is finished for the day and the vendors begin packing up their stands, tossing their rotten tomatoes, molding lemons, festering zucchini, and wilted greens onto the gray cobblestoned pavement. They leave hills of battered produce and mountains of the wooden crates used to haul their daily stocks from the city's wholesale market.

At that point, when the Campo looks like a garbage dump, cleanup crews—some plying medieval-looking willow brooms or plastic-fronded imitations, others maneuvering ultramodern street-washing trucks—vacuum up and hose down the chaos. Walk through the Campo about three p.m. and, except for a lingering smell of seafood on the eastern edge of the square, a visitor would have no idea that this was anything other than a large, lovely Roman piazza, about the size and shape of a football field, with a ceremonial fountain splashing at one end and a looming, hooded statue standing in its center.

At first glance Rome often seems all turmoil and frenzy. But time reveals a gentle side, too, a city of measured pace and rounded edges, a place not just of sun and heat, but of color and grace, whose comforts can outweigh its chaos. When we returned to Rome, ghostlike, in 1992, we were longing for those comforts, that blend of light, warmth, food, beauty, and friends—the very elixir that had nourished and protected us before our jobs as foreign correspondents called us off to cover the collapse of communism in Eastern Europe. We had taken a battering during our five years away. Italy seemed the place to try to get over it.

Both of us had lived essentially fortunate lives before we met in Rome in 1985, when I was thirty-four and John was forty-three. We lived four essentially joyous years afterward, deeply grateful to have found each other. Only then, just after the Berlin Wall fell in 1989, were we sucked into what I came to think of as our own private tornado. Though I don't believe the maxim that trouble comes in threes, I suspect that consecutive blows make it harder to rebound, easier to be dragged into a downward spiral. Our troubles began with a police truncheon in Czechoslovakia, two weeks before our wedding, and a bullet in Romania three weeks after. Infection, illness, and a family tragedy followed, and finally—the result of all that had come before—a long, slow slide into textbook depression.

I know that bad luck falls to everyone sooner or later. Ours simply hit especially hard, and lasted unusually long. This book recounts our troubles and how we found our way around them. It describes the simple strength we discovered in the one wild card we possessed: our love for Rome and the rituals we clung to there, all involving nourishment of one sort or another. These rituals of feeding and eating—rooted in our warmest memories from childhood and reinforced by our years in Italy—helped heal and strengthen us, allowed us to regroup. We cling to them still to ensure our future.

Like memory itself, this book wanders back and forth between old recollections and new. Food is the thread that connects them, for food has always been my lens and prism, my eye on the world. I may write about the smell of asparagus, the color of polenta, or the taste of figs still warm from the sun, but all of it is a personal shorthand for weighing hunger and love, health and nourishment, secrets and revelations, illness and survival, comfort and celebration, and perhaps above all, the joy and gift of being alive.

Can you love a city for its pink mornings and golden twilights? For the screech of its seagulls, the flitting of its swifts? Can you love a city because it is a riot of ochres and earth tones, all of them drenched by a fierce, rich light? Can you feel sheltered by the earth-hugging chaos of a city's skyline, exhilarated by its church domes floating like balloons across a deep blue sky? Can you feel nourished for a lifetime because an ancient city has never forgotten that its citizens need honest, fresh, and simple food, not only to survive but to flourish?

I know I loved Rome because of the water that streamed out my kitchen faucet, not only because it was clear and icy even in summer but because it sprang from the same mountain sources tapped by the engineers—or were they magicians?—of ancient

Rome. I know I never got over the first joyful shock of seeing live green acanthus growing near the Colosseum, in the shadows of columns that are topped by stone acanthus carved thousands of years ago. I know I felt I belonged the day my butcher, standing behind his pocked marble counter, asked if I was planning a *festa* when I ordered four, not two, scaloppine of pale, pink veal.

Rome took me in the first time I saw it, a stifling August night when I was thirty-two. I stumbled into a seat along the cool marble benches that ring the Trevi Fountain, a few steps from my hotel. Two elderly matrons in freshly ironed housedresses were taking their ease, fanning their bare arms and legs as they sat and chatted in the cool, damp air the fountain produced. Acknowledging my presence with a discreet nod of the head, they soon began peppering me with questions. When had I arrived? Two hours earlier. *Allora*, what did I think of the Colosseum, the Forum, the Palatine, San Pietro? The larger of the two eyed me incredulously when I said that the Trevi Fountain was the only thing I had seen. They stopped their fanning. They collected themselves, took each other by the arm, and walked me slowly the few blocks to Piazza Navona, describing the city's most elegant parlor with a pride of possession so strong that they themselves might have owned it. They left me there marveling in the pink-gold splendor of the square, whose three splashing fountains somehow swallow up the din of the city, leaving space only for its charms.

1 🙦 Hungers

Some mornings, beginning in March, I wake up hungering for green asparagus. It is a grown-up hunger, for I don't remember asparagus cravings before I was twelve or thirteen, when my father learned to braise them in butter under three or four leaves of dripping wet lettuce. The lettuce, lightly salted, would wilt, then give up a mild, sweet juice in which the asparagus would steam. When they were done and my father lifted the lid, a cloud of vegetable essence would fill the entire kitchen. My mother would sigh in delight at the smell of it, and even my brother, five or six at the time and still finicky in his appetites, would devour them. On those days, our hunger for asparagus was boundless.

Decades later, sudden unshakable hungers still seize me

throughout the year. In winter, it might be a craving for baby artichokes, braised in olive oil and mint, eaten barely warm. In spring I often crave strawberries—the smaller, the better—sliced over a mound of fresh ricotta. In summer I long for figs, or tomatoes, their juices still warm from the sun. In fall, I want and need a fat persimmon, quartered, opened up like a flower, sprinkled with lemon juice and eaten slowly, with ceremony and a spoon.

My maternal grandmother's Neapolitan soul knew and respected these sudden cravings. She called them *voglie*, an Italian word that can mean anything from wishes, wants, and desires to longings, fancies, or whims. But when Jennie Comparato used the word in Bridgeport, Connecticut, in the 1950s she meant only one thing—those deep, impulsive hungers for some special seasonal feast. The word is properly pronounced *VOHL-yay*, with the accent on the first syllable. But all of us in the family, none of whom had ever been to Italy, heard it rather differently. "*Wool-EEE*" is what we used to say, Americanizing it beyond recognition. We changed the *v* to a *w*, we changed the sound of the *o*, we accented the last syllable instead of the first.

"I've got the *wool-eee* for a cream cheese sandwich on date-nut bread," my mother might sigh on a particularly bleak Saturday morning in late January when she was convinced spring would never come again. If her *wool-eee* was serious, she would slap on lipstick and a hat and order me out of my flannel-lined dungarees and into a hated hand-me-down skirt. She would pop me into the backseat of the Olds and drive us downtown. There, in a wood-paneled bakery and sandwich shop called Harkabus, she would satiate her desire, sighing in quiet joy at her first bite, as if that mixture of brown bread and white cheese could coax the bare magnolia in the front yard into early bloom. I never shared her enthusiasm for that particular sandwich, and she never thought to press it. *Wool-eees* were personal, and though best when shared, could not be coerced. She satisfied her soul her way and I took care of mine, with bacon, lettuce, and tomato on toast, the mayonnaise carefully scraped off.

Jennie and the entire Comparato clan—she had seven brothers and sisters, four half brothers and half sisters—took *wool-eees* seriously, never mocking or ignoring these often inexplicable desires. When a *wool-eee* erupted, they knew the stomach was speaking. And the stomach, in our family, was to be listened to attentively, not just blindly fed. In our family the stomach was only slightly less important than the brain, and according to my mother, clearly more trustworthy and often more intelligent. I was not quite sure what she meant by those words nor by the fierceness of the tone she used when uttering similar pronouncements, all of which ended with a look into my eyes and the same tag line: "That's life—better get used to it."

I thought at the time, and for many, many years, that she was talking to me when she made those pronouncements that sounded so wise and so certain. Later I understood that she was talking mainly to herself. At any rate, by age six or seven, I knew *wool-eees* bespoke nourishment and need, both of body and of soul. I knew they transcended mundane treats. Neither body nor soul could ever pretend to require a Hostess Snowball, a lemon Popsicle, or an Almond Joy.

When I first moved to Rome, in my early thirties, it was the abundance of Roman *voglie* that made me feel welcome, almost as if I'd moved home. Romans have *voglie* for all manner of edible things. They are sometimes tied to the days of the week, like the need for potato gnocchi on Thursdays, or for thick pasta and chickpea soup, with rosemary and dried red pepper, on Fridays. They are sometimes tied to hours of the day, such as a craving for *spaghetti aglio, olio, e peperoncino* late at night or for a piece of warm *pizza bianca* on the way home from school. They are often tied to seasons of the year, when the body instinctively knows what it needs to eat, such as a mountain of midwinter spinach, barely warm and drizzled with olive oil and lemon; for ricotta in spring, when the cows and ewes produce their sweetest milk; for deep platters of mussels in white wine and garlic, all you can stand on a broiling summer night; for a brown paper cone of roasted chestnuts in November, just off one of the battered braziers that appear on street corners when cooler weather finally sets in.

Each year my own *wool-eees* grow stronger, as if by being satisfied they are heightened instead of diminished. It makes a certain sense, for if we are charmed once, and charmed again by repeating the performance, our memories hold the weight of both. So it is that toward the end of each succeeding winter, I need asparagus even more than I needed it the year before.

These days I find myself willing local asparagus into the market even before it is ready for harvest. By the time they actually arrive, I can almost taste them. But it is not just the taste I crave. I hunger as much, perhaps even more, for what their seasonal appearance signals: that the dark and cold and death of winter is about to yield to the sun and heat and promise of spring. I hunger then for their springy green color, for the sharp crack they make when I snap off the bottom of a muddy, fibrous, white-tipped stalk. I hunger, too, for the sight of them in an orderly, buttered mound, their sweet, blunt tips all pointing in the same direction, lying on a thick white pottery platter and covered with freshly grated Parmigiano-Reggiano cheese. I even hunger for the proof I have eaten them, for asparagus is the only vegetable I know that produces a vegetal, acrid smell in pee. I hunger, too, for that cloud of asparagus-lettuce perfume that used to fill our kitchen when I was twelve or thirteen, and the four of us ate them, happily.

In Rome, when I needed and wanted and simply had to have asparagus, I walked to Campo dei Fiori early to choose the pick of the lot. They would be standing upright on Signora Maria's crowded vegetable stall, wrapped in green-and-white paper, as if they were flowers, secured with a thick green rubber band so that only the fat tips showed. Back home, I would snap off the woody bottoms where they themselves knew to break. I would wash off the grit, then wish I didn't have to wait till dinner. Sometimes, if that wish was very strong, I didn't. I boiled a few right then and cooked them gently with a beaten egg to produce a filched asparagus frittata, which tastes better than anything, probably because its main ingredient has been stolen, for hunger's sake.

The first few times each season, I want them whole, with a bit of butter melting over them and lots of freshly grated Parmigiano. If John is traveling, I may balance my plate on my knees while sitting on my favorite stool, and this private kitchen picnic will be as satisfying as any proper meal at a well-set table. If John is in town, we'll sit at table, the platter between us, and stalk by stalk contentedly share my winter-to-spring *wool-eee*. Later in the season, for variety, I may dribble a bit of good green-gold olive oil over them while they are still warm. Just as I am about to eat, I squeeze a wedge of lemon over them, and the lemon oil gets into the skin of my fingers and into the air, and the lemon juice rides in droplets atop the olive oil, and the sweetness of the asparagus mingles with the oil and juice. It is a private, heady potion, my own call to Persephone to summon spring.

When I no longer need to eat them whole, I chop them into bits and pieces to turn them into spring's best risotto, using the asparagus water in which the stalks are first cooked as a mild, sweet broth that both colors and flavors the rice. It is a vegetable tonic, helping the body and mind make that longed-for but always difficult change of seasonal gears from darkness to light. In our house, risotto is always served from a large, deep oval platter, just as it appeared on the mahogany dining table in Jersey City when John was a boy. Risotto served from a bowl or from a flat, round plate doesn't taste right to him. When I appear with a platter of asparagus risotto, the color of the soft green cloud that hovers over a tree just before it bursts into leaf, neither of us is craving just the simple ingredients that went into the pot. For me, every forkful is like each bite my mother took from her cream cheese sandwich: a reassurance that winter will, in fact, finally end. For John, I think, each taste satisfies his longing for all the Tagliabues who ate supper together in the two-family house on Columbia Avenue, for Mother and Daddy; for the older boys, Charles, Robert, and Paul; for Aunt Julia, who never married; for Upstairs Grandma, who used to sing softly and absently for hours as she sat in her kitchen just above theirs.

When we returned to Rome after our years away, we arrived with another sort of craving, a hunger for normalcy, a *wool-eee* for some sort of old-fashioned cure. The treatment we sought, unconsciously at first, centered on food. Not fancy food or chichi restaurants, not the latest food fads or expensive ingredients. Just the magic of honest food—fresh and wholesome—simply prepared and eaten together three times a day, from ingredients that Italians have largely been eating for millennia. Italy still celebrates one of the most primordial rituals of the human community, the daily sharing of food and fellowship around a family table. What better place to take ourselves to heal?

Even before the troubles began raining down, we had begun

to paint Italy as a haven, a refuge, the place to recover from too much work. John was the Warsaw bureau chief for *The New York Times*, I was the Eastern European correspondent for the *Chicago Tribune*. Each summer, nearly played out, we would collect John's children, Peter and Anna, from Germany and return to the same magical house on the steep, scrub-covered hills in Trevignano Romano, a quiet village that overlooks Lake Bracciano, an hour's drive north of Rome.

We used to arrive, pale and wan, craving the sun, the heat, the food, the wine, the daily Monopoly games, the hours of reading, the afternoon swims, the naps on the beach, the nightly stroll on the lakeside promenade with ice cream dripping off our cones. We craved the trumpet vines that surrounded our bedroom windows and the cosseting of our older friends, Ann and Joseph, who had built two simple houses on the land, to use as a weekend retreat from the daily chaos of life in Rome. After three blissful weeks in Trevignano, we would leave tanned and rested, nearly restored. The best years, we arrived at the height of fig season, when a neighbor would leave enormous wicker baskets of green-gold figs on our back steps. Anna, seven or eight then, and I would stand around the basket and devour them, three and four at a go—our luggage, even the lake, forgotten. Nothing seemed to banish our hungers more than those meltingly soft figs oozing the thick, honeyed juice of an Italian summer.

After the troubles started, then multiplied and multiplied again, we stubbornly tried to keep to our ritual summer cure.

We flew to Rome, met the children, and drove back up to the lake. There were no fat figs on the steps that summer, though. The neighbor who had always welcomed us with the fruits of her tree had died suddenly, shortly before we arrived.

Even if I try to list the troubles simply, objectively, without elaboration, without a frame, I still sound to myself like one of those thin, nervous women—their lips working, their eyes not meeting the camera—who used to appear on *Queen for a Day* and tell their tales of woe. The woman with the most pitiful story and the most copious tears won the crown and the fur-trimmed robes. She won the long-stemmed roses, and maybe a refrigerator or some big cash prize. Under the crown and the robe, the winners would sob and laugh, cry and dissolve before the whirring camera. I watched that show with horror as a child, seeing grown-up terrors of loss and suffering paraded across the little octagonal screen of our first television set. It was a peculiar show for its time, oddly un-American, designed to reward trouble, to let a loser win. But I kept my horror of it well hidden, knowing the show would be forbidden if I let on how terrified it left me. I hated to watch it but hated to miss it, afraid this key to the grown-up world of troubles and fears might get away from me. If I watched, took in, and learned its secrets, maybe I could be ready for the adult terrors that obviously were waiting to be grown into, just like the bulky winter coat bought cheap at the end of the season for the following year's wear.

The troubles that, in fact, were waiting started in Prague on

November 17, 1989, the first night of what later came to be called the Velvet Revolution against the country's Communist leaders. Czechoslovak antiterrorist police waded into a peaceful crowd of student demonstrators and beat everyone in reach. I was there to report on it and they beat me unconscious in the street, then dragged me off with a colleague who had tried to intervene, hauling us into a building entryway, where they could continue to beat us, with impunity and without witnesses.

Five weeks later it was John's turn. Two nights before Christmas, a sniper hiding in the darkness of a city street in Timişoara, Romania, fired at the two-door Peugeot in which John was riding, shattering the car windows, tearing through doors, dashboard, seats, trunk, engine, and roof. The car was demolished, but neither the Frenchman at the wheel nor the two other Americans in the backseat were hit. John was struck by only one bullet, which he remembers "scurrying like a mouse" across his entire middle before he passed out.

I know that a riot stick connecting with a human target makes a sharp *thwack*ing sound when it hits a skull, and a slightly muffled, duller *thwock* when it hits flesh. I know that hundreds of shiny white plastic riot sticks catch and reflect streetlamps as they whoosh and flail like crazed metronomes in cold night air. I know what a gunshot sounds like. But I wasn't there when John was shot, so I can only wonder about the specifics of the scene. Was there a flash of white light when the sniper squeezed the trigger? Or maybe just a dirty yellow spark? I'd like to know if the bullet was spit out with a spike of blue smoke, or whether a puff of gray fume wafted lazily up into the December night. Had I been standing hard by, would I have heard the bullet cut the air? Would it have whined or screamed or whispered or made no sound at all?

I needed fifteen simple stitches to close the two long gashes in my head and a couple of weeks for my hugely swollen face to look again like mine. Had my beating been the sum of it, I probably would have nursed a longtime fear of uniformed men wielding riot sticks, but would have few other lingering concerns. But a bullet that pierces a car door, a parka, a sports coat, a sweater, a shirt, trousers, and underwear—a bullet that splits a belt in two, then chews its way across a body I knew and loved—causes an entirely different level of injury. The body is only the first victim; the soul, the psyche, the spirit are each ripped apart as well. People who had learned this lesson in their own particular ways—a wise hospital orderly in Munich, friends who had lost a child, an acquaintance who had once been knifed in the chest— tried to warn us early on that our lives would never be quite the same. They tried to let us know that any biography-changing trauma such as a car wreck or a heart attack was likely to split a life in two, into the time before and the time after.

But we weren't ready to take in their wisdom. It was only over the years that we began to understand that the troubles that befall us alter, permanently, not only our view of the world but our position in it. We still had so very much to learn. Who would have thought that patience could be a vice? And anger a virtue? Who would have thought that there are times when it is not only natural to feel angry and impatient but of enormous importance to demand that a sick person show signs of getting better? Who would have thought that the most fundamental of human rituals—buying, preparing, eating, and sharing our daily bread—would have become our tether to normal life as we struggled to make the crossing from our old life before to our new life after?

The Romanian surgeon who first saved John's life said the bullet slammed into his right side, shattering his pelvis and sending shards of bone deep into the surrounding muscles. The German surgeons who saved his life later said the bullet then tumbled and danced its way across the rest of him, skimming close enough under his spine to shatter the tip of one vertebra and slightly fracture two more. Ultimately, though, it skimmed under his spinal column and chewed across the rest of him, exiting his left side just above what was left of his belt. Doctors— first in Timişoara, and later in Munich—had to cut open John's back to expose and clean the tunnel the bullet had made. They had to clean out the bits of bone, metal, paint, dirt, grease, and shredded cloth that the bullet carried with it. They had to kill the inevitable infection that followed, and weeks later, when there was enough new flesh to stitch, they had to sew up the long, deep trench—about as wide and deep as my forearm— that they and the bullet had made.

No one ever found the bullet that found John, so the experts were forced to theorize about what exactly hit him. The Romanian doctors thought it was a dumdum, a soft-nosed bullet that expands upon hitting a target so as to produce maximum damage as it travels through the body. One of the Munich surgeons, an avid hunter, said the bullet may have been absolutely ordinary, but that the impact of bullet against car door, bullet against pelvic bone, so destabilized its course that it mimicked the malignant bob and weave of a dumdum.

Whatever it was, we still have a fabric footprint of how and where the bullet slipped in. Romanian hospital workers somehow managed to save most of John's clothes despite the bloody bedlam of an ill-equipped hospital emergency room inundated with casualties when the revolution erupted in Timişoara a few days earlier. The staff wrapped John in his parka before our emergency flight to Munich, and he actually wore it a couple of times the following winter, but only till we managed to replace it. The holes were too noticeable, too disquieting, and we finally threw that parka out. We stashed his sports jacket and khakis out of sight in an old wooden cupboard. Later, I cut them up, saving a few square inches around the holes where the bullet slipped in. Then I stuffed them into a drawer along with everything else I had saved from the shooting, enough to fill a four-inch-thick binder.

If I pull the swatches out of the file, I can see two raggedy holes in the herringbone tweed where the bullet entered the bunched-up sports jacket. Far clearer is the single hole in the khakis, perfectly centered on the seam where waistband meets trousers, directly above the right rear pocket. I used to look at these bits of cloth occasionally, as if they could tell me what had happened and why. But no matter how many times I looked, the holes refused to speak.

Years later, I still have difficulty even connecting them to a shooting. Shootings, I still like to think, happen to drug dealers or innocent passersby in New York, to foreign tourists visiting Miami. They happen to people who clean guns or keep them under their beds. They happen to soldiers, to policemen, to mafiosi, to people who have enemies. They don't happen to my husband, my family, to me. I suspect my response of utter disbelief is standard for anyone who hasn't been blindsided by some sort of shock: the sudden diagnosis of a rampaging cancer, the overnight loss of a family's life savings. Shocks like these hammer home the notion that a history of good luck is no amulet for the future.

2 ❧ Eating Out

In some ways, I think a move to Italy was destined to be as much in my future as a move from Italy had been in my family's past. As a child, I moved only once, from the Fairfield side of Ash Creek to the Bridgeport side. We went from a two-bedroom flat we rented to a three-bedroom house we owned; from a lumbering two-family house overlooking a reedy marsh full of red-winged blackbirds to a two-story, single-family colonial, whose western windows looked out over the broad expanse of a saltwater tidal basin full of gulls. I was nine, my brother, Danny, two, and my mother always said that we spent that entire first day clattering up and down the straight wooden staircase that led to our new, separate bedrooms.

My parents never dreamed of moving again, and my brother

still lives an hour away from the old house, but it seems the delight that took hold of me that first moving day left me hungry to move on. Family history played a role, too. My family had started out in Italy; at some elemental level I needed to go back, to see what they had left and why, to see what my life might have been like had my grandparents or their families not packed their trunks and gone to *l'America*.

My first move on my own, to college just west of Boston, was the bliss of freedom. The move to a cramped apartment in Hartford, Connecticut, nearly four years later, to marry, was all joy. The move to a quirky flat in the top story of a historic house in Plainville, Connecticut, was magic, especially when I landed my first reporting job at a nearby newspaper. The move to a Dallas suburb three years later—during an endless New England cold spell that left me shivering in our thin-walled, insulation-free apartment—was a revelation: one could actually avoid winter, forever, with something as simple as a move.

My next move, alone, to an old neighborhood of down-at-the-heel wooden houses in Dallas itself, was painful but right. My six-year-old marriage had long been dying, and a judge was about to grant the divorce my first husband had sought. The house that I spent the next three years restoring was my psychologist. I hammered, sanded, patched, painted, laid floors and sub-floors, ordered wallpaper, planted iris, staked tomatoes, picked green beans, and tended herbs in a heat so intense that my basil plants grew waist high. I could rock to and fro in one of my old front-veranda swings and smell the basil baking in the sunshine or the figs drying on the branches of the old tree that kept the sun at bay.

It didn't bother me that I no longer had a bed, and was sleeping on foam camping mats on the restored parquet flooring of my new bedroom. With a window seat as my headboard, I lay happily under twelve-foot ceilings and a glittering crystal chandelier that had been so obscured by sixty-five years of grime and dust that I initially thought it was made of black plastic.

My mother came to visit shortly after I moved in, to make sure I was surviving the divorce proceedings, the first in our family. It was a singular moment, with a certain fragility hanging in the air, not only because neither of us dared bicker with the other for the few days we were together. I was twenty-eight, she sixty-one, and over a long pot of tea and slices of apple cake at an old-style café not far from downtown, she told me a story I had never heard, a story that, in a heartbeat, seemed to explain the central puzzle of my childhood. Her story, though I didn't know it at the time, would also prepare me in some ways for what was to come later in my life with John.

Squeezing lemon into her tea, she spoke in a confessional tone I had never before heard her use. She told me she had developed the baby blues after my birth. Not the normal come-and-go baby blues but the kind that come and stay. This being the 1950s, and my mother never given to revelations, she kept her illness secret, except for the family. Her older sister, Marie, would call her daily to try to get her to stop sobbing. Auntie would talk and talk, telling her to put on her coat and hat, dress me warmly, pop me into my carriage, and get out into the fresh air. My mother usually managed to follow her sister's advice, day after day pushing the carriage across the Ash Creek bridge into Black Rock, tears rolling down her cheeks, her favorite epithet, "sonofabitch," escaping softly, in whispers, into the air.

The only professional advice she remembered receiving came from the doctor who delivered me. "He clapped me on the shoulder," she said, her voice still shaking with rage and emotion nearly three decades later. "He clapped me on my shoulder and told me to buck up," she said. "'You've got a nice baby there to take care of. Get on with it.'" She tried, heroically, it seems to me now. And with my father pitching in when he got home from work, and my mother's parents pitching in while he was at the office, and my aunt playing psychologist by phone and in person, time went by. Still terribly ill by the time I turned two, she underwent electroshock therapy, done as an outpatient procedure in those days, and soon she came around.

She told me that a miscarriage a couple of years later sent her back for more shock treatments, after six months of depression. A second miscarriage provoked the same response, the same treatment. My brother's birth, seven years after mine, provoked a yearlong collapse, she said, but a last round of shock treatments brought her out of it again.

I sat across from her, our cake plates empty, our teacups

drained. I had no memories of anything she had related. Nonetheless, the puzzle pieces of my childhood suddenly seemed to find their place. Much as she loved me, she found me a source of both joy and pain. My birth had made her a mother; my birth had made her insane. Her story explained her shakiness, her anger, her mood swings, our complicated mother-daughter life, my uneasiness in her presence, the reason I disliked hugging her. Had I known all this earlier, I would not have had to fight so hard to keep her at bay.

"Why didn't you tell me sooner?" I asked, without a trace of my usual pique.

"Because I was afraid you wouldn't want to have children," she said. She paused a moment, looking at the crumbs left on the solid, white café china. Then she looked up. "Having children is the best," she said, taking a breath. "And the worst."

Two years earlier, in 1977, my first husband and I had moved to Texas so that I could take a job with United Press International. My salary more than doubled—providential, since my husband was out of work—but it was UPI's nature as an international news agency that interested me most, for it meant the chance of a transatlantic posting sometime in the future. Dallas back then was a tight, closed world so provincial that a local, university-educated colleague was deeply shocked the day he learned I was a Catholic, despite my blue eyes and dirty-blond hair. "Darlin'," he muttered, "you sure don't look Mezkin." After five years in Dallas—and three weeks after I finished restoring my beloved old house—I finally got the first of the transatlantic transfers I had been hoping for. Within months I was living alone in London, editing UPI copy from Europe, the Middle East, and Africa and helping cover, at a distance, Britain's improbable war over the Falkland Islands. I was thirty-two. Later UPI transferred me to Madrid and then back to London before bouncing me, a year later, to Rome, a city I so loved I was not sure I could ever leave.

I would probably be living there now if I had not met John late in the summer of 1985. Long based in Bonn, the former West German capital, John was on a yearlong assignment in Rome. We met in passing on a broiling August day at an outdoor pool where foreign reporters could swim practically for free. A couple of weeks later we met again, when a small group of mutual friends got together at a restaurant whose terrace, crammed with vines and plants, enjoyed the slight breeze that often descends upon Rome late of an August evening. My brother, visiting from Connecticut, was with me that night, as was Lou, a writer and English professor who was one of my closest friends. Both of them took to John that evening as easily as I did.

My brother had to fly back to the States the next day, but Lou was with me a week later when John made good on his offer to cook everybody one of his mother's best risottos. The recipe started out like a *risotto alla milanese*, made with butter, onion, rice, chicken broth, saffron, and Parmigiano, but ended up enriched with dried porcini mushrooms and skinny *luganega* sausage cut into what John described as "Tootsie Roll-sized pieces."

Wedged into the narrow galley kitchen of a colleague, John seemed utterly at home as he whipped up the meal, sidling from countertop to stove and doling out joke instructions: insisting that the onions be cut just so, wheedling for a bit of red wine for the cook, and suddenly breaking into a mad whistling as he began to grate the Parmigiano. "You absolutely *have* to whistle while grating the cheese," he announced, raking the cheese across an old-fashioned hand grater and explaining that in a household with four large, hungry boys and a very large, hungry father, Parmigiano always had a way of mysteriously disappearing during the grating process in their Jersey City kitchen. His mother, he said, could only keep to her budget if she required her helpers to whistle as they grated, for as long as they were whistling, they could not be eating it when her back was turned.

John, who had tucked a dish towel into his trouser waistband to serve as an apron, cooked a huge batch of risotto that night, and Lou and I and the other friends who were there finished it off in short order, marveling that none of us had ever eaten a risotto like it before. When somebody murmured that she was full, John responded without missing a beat, "Barrels are full. *You* have had sufficient." He looked at us and laughed: "Chapter three, verse two, May Tagliabue's own Bible of personal rules of behavior."

Since my own kitchen was minuscule, with no oven and just two tiny gas burners, Lou offered to host a similar meal a week or two later so that I could make good on my offer to make the group one of my family's favorite dishes, *gnocchi verdi*—tiny, light dumplings made with ricotta and spinach—served with a mild, buttery tomato sauce enriched with a bit of cream. Late one night we all crowded into Lou's small kitchen while I made the gnocchi dough. John pitched in to help with the messy job of forming cherry-sized gnocchi in the floured palms of our hands. Laughing and chatting easily, we rolled and rolled the sticky dough in tiny balls as flour flew in all directions. Even Lou, fastidious to a fault, agreed the floury mess on his counter-top and floor was easily worth the taste.

Maybe it was John's Jersey accent or his help in the kitchen that so reminded me of home. Maybe it was his innate gentle-ness or the kindness and light I saw in his eyes. Maybe it was that he looked like a cross between Alan Alda and my mother's cousin Tom, or that his face was as boyish as his too-short chi-nos. Whatever it was, all I knew was that within a few weeks, for the first time since my divorce six years earlier, I felt drawn to a man instead of wanting to flee; felt promise, not fear.

John and I first came to know each other over what seems now like an endless series of dinner tables, most of them set on the cobblestones outside simple Roman trattorie, because when one works until ten or eleven or midnight, night after night, movies or concerts or museums are not real options. So after

John had finished filing his nightly story and after I had closed the UPI bureau, we fell into the habit of meeting up with other reporter friends for late, light, cheap suppers of honest food and nonstop conversation.

It was here—over tables covered in white butcher paper, tables that wobbled on the uneven cobblestones, over small pitchers of Rome's trademark sour white wines—that John and I watched and listened to each other kibitzing with friends, where we first dared to open up to each other. We would talk and eat, eat and talk, for hours, all under makeshift roofs of giant white canvas *ombrelloni*, oversized parasols that spout like mushrooms outside so many Roman restaurants.

We might talk about the day's news, Italian politics, Vatican pronouncements, boneheaded editors, whatever new archaeological or architectural details we might have discovered that day, for *bella Roma* is an endless trove of nooks and crannies filled with visual treasures just waiting to be noticed during a morning stroll to the market or the office: a tiny fountain in the shape of a foot-long barrel tucked into the façade of an otherwise nondescript palazzo; the ornately carved capital of an ancient Roman column peeking out of a pockmarked, dirty wall.

Working our way through small bowls of spaghetti with fresh baby clams, or a small grilled sea bass, a mound of barely cooked spinach, or bowls of tiny blueberries, raspberries, and currants, we would talk, listen, debate, argue, regale. John, who had studied and taught Latin at Bonn University and worked at an institute of medieval Latin for years before becoming a reporter, had a way of mixing the erudite with the goofy, going on at length in pig Latin, then bringing in a few lines from Horace or Virgil to hammer his point home. Once the cooling night air signaled it would soon be time to end the evening, his jokes would start coming. John would somehow manage to get us laughing at his father's oldest, corniest jokes—What was the head singing as it floated down the Hudson River? "I ain't got no-body," he would warble—before we settled our bills and adjourned.

When I recall those evenings, I always think of that magical moment, hours after sunset, when Rome's night breezes began blowing out the hot, stale air of the day, when that curious mix of city streetlamps, car headlights, and restaurant lanterns started casting a magical pink-gold light across a seventeenth-century palazzo's crumbling ochre walls or over a Baroque façade half hidden by a wall of ivy or Virginia creeper. The sensation I had of having eaten well, of having talked away the burdens of the day, of having laughed and joked and relaxed, of having felt embraced and supported by food and drink and talk and companionship, unconsciously brought to mind those comforting meals I used to eat—day after day, year after year—around my family's kitchen table.

One night after a long, lazy supper out with friends, John and I decided to take a walk on the Pincio, a steep, high ridge on the edge of the Borghese Gardens that looks west across the center of Rome toward the Tiber and beyond to the enormous dome of St. Peter's. It has been a magical view, I would guess, since the days of the emperors, when the ancients strolled through the same sort of pleasure gardens, then known as the Horti Pinciani. We stood on the broad lookout of the Pincian parapet, where even without moonlight we could make out dozens of church cupolas, St. Peter's great dome the most visible of all. We stood, content, gazing across Rome's night skyline and picked out the domes we could most easily identify, the ziggurat top of Sant'Ivo alla Sapienza, the broad, flattish dome of the ancient Pantheon, the grand dome of Santa Maria del Popolo, which rose literally at our feet.

I remember that night we sat, content, on a green park bench as words tumbled out of us willy-nilly in a way neither of us had experienced before. John told me about the wooden astrolabe, quadrant, and sextant he had built when he was nine or ten after founding a club, the Junior Men of the Sea, and how he and his friends would climb his garage roof in Jersey City to try to sight the North Star. In turn, I told him about the fishing lines my sixth-grade friend Jeannie and I would cast into Long Island Sound when the snapper blues were running, and how we would scream with joy when those tiny voracious bluefish would seize the raw bacon we had used as bait.

John told me about his father, who could be the life of the party one moment, sad and teary the next. I told him about my mother, another life of the party, who loved to push away her fears on a ballroom dance floor.

John told me how filled with joy he had been during his first three years as a young monk in a Trappist monastery just after high school. He told me how he had fallen into a depression during his last year at the monastery, how electroshock treatments had helped bring him round, how bereft he felt later when he returned to the world outside the abbey walls. His talk of beating depression, given my mother's history, only made him feel more familiar.

I told him how full of joy and promise I too had been when I first married, and how deeply I had longed for a passel of children, preferably boys, to avoid another complicated mother-daughter life. I told him how bereft I too had felt later, when I first realized that my marriage had irretrievably failed. I told him about lying on my back in bed, awake and alone one awful night in Dallas years earlier, when I suddenly realized that the thought of having children with my first husband brought only cold horror, not joy, to my mind. I told him how my left arm had been half hanging off the edge of that unhappy bed and how I felt as if my blood and soul had drained out of my dangling fingertips, and with them, the marriage and the children I had once hoped to have.

We were still sitting on that green park bench when I finished speaking, and as I looked at John I felt a sorrow deep inside me dislodge. The horror of that Dallas night began to melt, the sadness that had settled in with the horror fading away, too.

Suddenly the tall, thin, brown-haired man with the kind

brown eyes who was sitting beside me on that green park bench seemed utterly familiar, as if I had known him for decades. Suddenly, seamlessly, we seemed to be talking about the future, our future, together.

John remembers experiencing that same sense of familiarity just after we met, a feeling that after years of trying, he had finally come home. "I knew very quickly that wherever you were would be home," he wrote to me recently. "That's been true even after twenty years and more."

I know I came to love John because he wrote chatty letters home to his mother every week, because even in his forties he called her "Mother"; because he still referred to his father, long dead, as "Daddy." I came to love him because he never stopped talking about his parents, three brothers, grandparents, aunts, uncles, cousins, nieces, and nephews, and above all, about his children, Peter and Anna. I came to love him because his family was enormous, as mine once had been.

As time passed I loved him because he spoke broadly and listened deeply, because I knew he would never bore me, no matter how long we lived. I loved him because he could speak English, Italian, German, Spanish, French, and Latin, because he could read ancient Greek and a smattering of Hebrew. I loved him because he could not read music, but could read and sing Gregorian chant. I loved him because he was not afraid of tears, his own or mine. I loved him because he grew up eating not just pasta but also, like my family, polenta, that cheap, yellow cornmeal mush that kept generations of northern Italian peasants from starving. I loved him because he loved the two children he had, and because he told me he wished he could give me a child, too.

I loved John also because, like me, he liked to cook as much as he liked to eat, because both of us grew up in homes where honest food was the central magnet that brought us all to the same table two or three times a day. I loved him because both of us were blessed with a metabolism that let us eat with pleasure, not guilt. I loved him also because both our families came to the table not just to eat, but to talk, laugh, share our problems, share our lives. I loved him because I could envision a lifetime of ordinary meals together, alone or with good friends who might share our sense of what nourishment really means. I loved him because he knew that good talk, good books, good music were one staff of life, and that simple, good food, shared with others, was the second. I loved him because he was smart enough to know that food was a lot more than fuel.

That both of us were working as foreign correspondents made our courtship easier, for only another reporter (or perhaps an obstetrician) could understand completely that when the job called, all other life went on hold. Even though John was in Rome for much of the next year, neither of us ever spent much time in the same place. Much of our courtship was, in fact, spent apart, because of the nature of the daily news business. Long and short absences were, from the beginning, part of our life together. Even before John returned to Bonn, we were used to depending on telegrams, letters, cards, telephones, and telexes—a clunky, international communications service dating back to the 1930s that sent and received hand-punched messages by teleprinter—to stay in touch. I have a file full of yellowing messages sent from wherever John happened to be working that remind me how happy we both were to have found each other, how the knowledge of each other's existence was enough to keep happy two people who had for years been feeling essentially alone. That we were usually in different cities or countries did not seem an insurmountable problem, as long as we knew the other could be reached by written or spoken word.

About eighteen months after we met, John's editors in New York named him Warsaw bureau chief. Even better, the *Times* gave him five months off from reporting duties to learn Polish. Overjoyed at the opportunity of actually being paid to learn a new language, John threw himself into intensive, one-on-one language studies with a Polish university student eight hours a day, six days a week.

His classes were scheduled to end in August 1987, two years after we had met, and when he asked me to marry him and move to Poland with him, I did not hesitate to accept. It meant giving up the UPI job that had brought me to Europe, but I would happily freelance in order to be with John—and then, serendipitously, I was hired by the *Chicago Tribune* as Eastern European correspondent. The wedding we initially envisioned in Warsaw would turn out to be bureaucratically impossible, but I see that now as providential. Our wedding ended up being celebrated—four years after we had met—in Rome, where we would eventually return, much sooner than we'd ever dreamed, to find sustenance and strength at a time of seemingly endless woe. It seemed right that the place that initially brought us together, as friends, lovers, and then as man and wife, would also be the place that held us together through our later trials.

3 ✤ Abbondanza *and* Nie Ma

To my mother's everlasting dismay, I was born scrawny. My brother, seven years later, was born scrawny, too. My mother herself was scrawny, most of her life, and my father even scrawnier, most of his. But rather than see her children's scrawniness as genetically expectable, she took it as reproof. Her vision of babyhood was plumpness and robustness: babies with dimpled knees and elbows—pillows of flesh where kisses could be dispensed. Our bony limbs never fulfilled her dreams. Into her seventies, she would still utter the same lament that greeted our arrival at the hospital decades earlier. How come, she would say, all my friends got beautiful, chubby babies? So how come, she would say, I got two plucked chickens?

I wonder now if it was this chasm between babies dreamed and babies born that made food and our ingesting of it so critical to her. Somewhere along the line she must have come up with the idea that if she could plump us up, fill us out, she would fulfill some primal requirement of good mothering. But if we stayed thin, if we followed her own childhood example of picking at our food, refusing milk, eating only what we felt like eating, God himself would brand her as eternally unworthy, an unspeakable failure.

Those last weeks in Rome were chaos as I tried to finish work, pack up my apartment, and figure out how to keep us fed in the years we would be behind the Iron Curtain. We knew Poland's food supplies were erratic, and that basics taken for granted anywhere in Western Europe either were not available in Poland or showed up so infrequently that they could not be counted on.

I had recently returned from a weeklong trip to Poland, crisscrossing the country during Pope John Paul II's third visit to his homeland. While in Warsaw I had slipped into a small grocery store to see what we were in for. The shop was a dreary void of mostly empty shelves peopled by weary clerks constantly muttering the same phrase, *Nie ma*, which means "There isn't any." Flour? "*Nie ma*." Sugar? "*Nie ma*." Pepper? "*Nie ma*." Having seen that market, where a few jars of strawberry jam were spread across six feet of shelf space, where eight pickle jars, each standing a foot apart, were occupying another section of otherwise empty shelving, where the only shelves that looked crowded were the ones bearing cans of tripe stew or bottles of cloudy vinegar, I took our colleagues' advice about stocking up.

In the weeks before we left Rome, I spent hours with our corner grocer, who ran a hole-in-the-wall shop in the valley between the Palatine and Capitoline hills. Roberto delivered endless cases of spaghetti, spaghettini, penne, fusilli, tiny stars of soup pasta, short, stubby Arborio rice for risottos, long-grain rice for other dishes, canned tomatoes, tuna and anchovies, olive oil, red-wine vinegar, fifteen-pound wedges of Parmigiano-Reggiano and pecorino cheeses, bags of dried *funghi porcini*, olives, jars of pesto, of artichoke hearts in olive oil, of baby onions in vinegar, of eggplant salads. I bought whole salamis, canisters of teas and coffees, and simple wines.

I spent some $1,500 in the weeks before we moved, mainly on food but also on other basics, such as toilet paper, paper towels, dishwashing soap, laundry powder, bath soap, toothpaste, shampoo, and standard cleaning products. Our shipment was full of seed packets, too: basil, parsley, zucchini, green beans, and arugula. But the following spring most of our Italian seeds proved too fragile for Poland's continental climate, and only the parsley and the arugula, a hearty, bitter salad green that is nearly impossible to kill, ever thrived in our tiny back garden. The other seeds sprouted but refused to grow.

Although our shipment of personal goods—a few bits of furniture, clothes, and housewares—looked more like the commercial move of a grocery store than the private move of a domestic household, my purchases were not nearly enough to last the years we were there. After the first few months, anytime John or I passed through a Western country, we would replenish our dwindling supplies and stagger back through Polish customs, like the Poles themselves, carrying bulging shopping bags. Ours were filled with tins of olive oil, cases of Italian pasta, or a couple of juicy, fresh pineapples.

I know it was those empty grocery shelves I had seen during my last papal trip that made me want to record the *abbondanza* I would be leaving behind. If I had to choose a single word to describe my life in Rome, *abbondanza*—which means "abundance, plenty, copiousness"—is the word that springs to mind. In Italian a cornucopia is a *corno dell'abbondanza*, our English horn of plenty. To roll in wealth in Italian is to swim *nell'abbondanza*. Eating one of Sicily's signature dishes, *caponata*, is a lesson in *abbondanza*, for the purple-black eggplants, the pale green celery, the white onions, the red bell peppers, the dark gray-green capers, the black olives, all cooked in oil, doused with a trace of sugar and a splash of red-wine vinegar, produce a dish of extraordinary beauty as well as taste, the individual colors of the vegetables taking on the beauty of bold stained glass.

I already knew I would never live in a more beautiful location. My roof terrace, three times as big as my tiny apartment, was drenched in sunlight and covered in monster terra-cotta pots of geraniums, cosmos, oleander, bay laurel, and sage. I already knew I would never again have such extraordinary views, for I looked up to the Palatine Hill, where the ancient Roman emperors used to live, to the Capitoline Hill, where they used to govern, and to the Aventine Hill, still a tree-covered oasis of calm in the city's historic center where ancient Roman aristocrats once built their homes. I already knew that my terrace could never be matched. How I loved its terra-cotta tiles, its dependable breezes, its faded canvas tarp that protected the big table and comfortable chairs where I ate all my meals, read all my books, spent all my waking hours. The terrace was where John, who loves to dance, would scoop me into his arms and waltz me around in the moonlight, the sunlight, or the occasional rain; where John, mid-waltz, was sure to whisper in my ear one of his standard old jokes: "Waltz a little faster, dear, they're playing a fox-trot."

Unconsciously perhaps, I also knew that the *abbondanza* of Rome's outdoor markets was the other thing I was sure to miss once the tiny moving van that was taking our few bits of furniture, clothes, and household gear to Warsaw arrived. The morning before moving day, I took a notebook instead of a shopping bag to the Campo dei Fiori and wrote down everything on offer at one of the more modest stands in the square. A truck farmer named Domenico presided over that stand, and much of what he sold he grew himself.

On that sunny August morning, Domenico was selling fat, round heads of soft Bibb lettuce and wild-looking heads of curly endive. He had crates of romaine lettuce, whose elongated heads form the base of many salads, and tight little knobs of red radicchio, to add color. He had fistfuls of wild arugula, which the Romans call *rughetta* and use to add a peppery bite to a meal. He had foot-long bunches of Swiss chard, tiny new shoots of broccoli rabe, bunches of slim scallions. He had bouquets of zucchini flowers, which Romans stuff with mozzarella and anchovy, dip in a light flour-and-water batter, then deep-fry till golden.

He had flat, green broad beans, the kind the Romans stew slowly in garlic, onion, and tomato. He had red and white runner beans, which housewives use to fill out a summer vegetable soup, and regular green beans, tiny, just picked, perfect for blanching and serving with a dribble of olive oil and lemon juice. Domenico also had the usual array of tomatoes, each with specific uses: tiny cherry tomatoes, so good halved and turned into a Neapolitan-style sauce; meaty, plum tomatoes used for endless tomato-based pasta sauces; salad tomatoes, always slightly green, as the Romans prefer them. He had Casilino tomatoes, too—small, flat, highly creased, with a sunlit, concentrated flavor, favored by Roman housewives for raw sauces during summer's worst heat. He had gigantic beefsteak tomatoes, too, meant for stuffing and baking with rice, potato wedges, oil, and herbs.

That day, Domenico was also selling carrots, celery, cucumbers, lemons. He had skinny frying peppers and fat bell peppers—red, yellow, and green—which the Romans love to roast and serve with oil and garlic. He had yellow- and red-skinned potatoes and the tough cow corn that Europeans seem to think people as well as cows can eat. He had fat, glossy, black-skinned eggplants, and long, narrow white ones with bright purple markings near the stem. He had hot red *peperoncini*, tiny peppers still on the stalk and ready for drying, and several types of zucchini, some a deep, dark green, others light and striated, none of them much bigger than an American hot dog, all sweet and free of seeds because of their tiny size. He was selling round yellow onions, sweet red onions, and flat white onions. He had garlic and fennel bulbs, their feathery tips a dark, cool green. He also had eggs, brown-shelled, as the Romans favor them, their shells never quite as clean as a shopper would hope.

Domenico had nectarines and peaches, too, yellow-fleshed and white. He had the tiny figs, some green, some purple, known as *settembrini*, or "little September ones," to distinguish them from the first growth of larger figs that appear in June. He had dark purple grapes; fat, round green grapes nearly as big as apricots; and long, narrow seedless grapes, always slightly tart. He had cantaloupes, some with smooth, green skins, others with veined yellow rinds, both with bright orange flesh. He also had bright yellow melons, whose white flesh lasts long after cantaloupes have gone by. He had watermelons, red plums, yellow plums, blue plums. He had yellow apples, green apples, and even a few red ones. He had case after case of prickly pears, so full of spines that they're best eaten with gloves.

And of course he had just-picked herbs—parsley, basil, sage, rosemary, and *mentuccia*, the small-leafed wild mint that Roman cooks often use to flavor artichokes or lamb. At any Italian market, sellers toss in these *odori* for free once a customer has completed his or her purchases. At the Campo, the usual *odori* included a carrot, a stalk of celery, a fistful of flat-leaf parsley, a sprig or two of rosemary, and—unless it is the dead of winter, when it must be greenhouse-grown, at great expense—several stalks of basil.

I stood in front of Domenico's U-shaped stand and wrote down what he was selling that broiling, sunny morning. He never used to carry any of the dozens of fancy or exotic fruit and vegetables some vendors stock—no avocados, mangos, blueberries, or ginger. But the bounty of Italy's growing season seems endless, and clearly visible in even a simple stand, where produce, piled high in wooden crates, is generally so fresh, bright, clean, and colorful, that it begs to be bought and eaten.

Three days later (unaware that Warsaw shoppers tended to patronize private farm stands for their fresh produce) I walked into the state-run produce shop not far from our new home in the Polish capital. Cramped, dreary, and grimy, the shop reeked of decaying vegetables, stale cigarette smoke, and ammonia. Two bored clerks did their best to ignore their customers and their surroundings. Most of the meager offerings of vegetables and fruit looked bruised, battered, tired, old. Considering it was still high summer, the offerings seemed so shockingly meager that I began to wonder if I had missed some declaration of war.

The shop was selling only a handful of items, virtually all of them root vegetables: dirt-encrusted potatoes; stubby, dirt-encrusted carrots; bunch after bunch of muddy beets; dirt-encrusted parsnips, celery root, horseradish, and onions; a few heads of exhausted lettuce; bright red salad radishes, nearly the only dirt-free item on offer; and plastic containers filled with fat cabbages, the only thing in the shop that looked as if it had been picked within recent memory. The fruit, if anything, looked even worse than the vegetables: battered brown-skinned apples, bruised green pears.

Roman housewives are extraordinarily particular about each ingredient they buy for the family pot. Haranguing the occasional vendor who might try to slip a less-than-perfect tomato into their sack is an art form of elevated nature. Had Roman housewives been transported to Warsaw en masse after the war, I thought, they surely would have staged violent, impromptu revolutions at their local greengrocers and the Communists might have been turned out of power decades earlier.

Our last night in Rome before the move, our closest friends organized a small, going-away dinner on the Gianicolo, a steep, verdant hill that overlooks the city spread out at its feet. We ate at one of our favorite outdoor restaurants, a large, noisy eatery set under vine-covered terraces whose vast array of antipasti alone was enough for a meal. We ate and drank, ate and talked, ate and laughed, ate and joked. My Greek-American friend, Eleni, was the only one who cried. Married to an Italian and unlikely ever to leave, she wept that she was being abandoned yet again by another peripatetic friend whom she had hoped would stay forever.

Around midnight, we all walked down the hill and across the Tiber to the Trevi Fountain, the very spot where I so happily started my life in Rome four years earlier. With our backs to Neptune and the leaping cascades of water through which he drives his imaginary chariot, John and I threw the prescribed coins over our left shoulders into the foaming fountain to ensure our return to Rome. Both of us knew the gesture was overkill; there was no question but that we would be back.

We stepped off our Alitalia flight to Warsaw the next day with suitcases slung over our shoulders and potted herbs in our hands. I carried the rosemary bush that had flavored so many of our Roman meals. John toted a terra-cotta pot of foot-high basil, planted specially that spring and coddled over the summer so that we could bring the taste of our old home to our new one.

We were still descending the plane's metal stairway to the tarmac when Warsaw suddenly seemed a very long way from Rome.

It was not just the cold, blustery summer rain drumming down, the type of weather that might occasionally blow into Rome in late November. Our two-and-a-half-hour flight seemed to have carried us over decades as well as miles, to some twilight period just after the war, a war that Italy clearly had won. It was a war that Poland just as clearly had lost, or that forty years later was somehow still dragging on, history be damned. Suddenly I was relieved we had decided to lug the herbs.

The air itself gave off a peculiar smell, an acrid, smoky sulfuric stink I had never smelled before. It came from the cheap, soft brown coal, full of sulfur and other pollutants, that heated homes, factories, and water from Vladivostok to the Fulda Gap. But there was more than a stink to the air. Weariness and resignation hung there, too, both more palpable than any chemical smell.

It took some months for me to realize that our move to Warsaw was more than a shift from West to East, more than a change from democracy to communism, more than a descent from first world to second. Moving from *bella Roma* to Warsaw was essentially a move from a world of sunny, golden *abbondanza* to a darker, drabber world of *nie ma*. From abundance to want, in one short flight.

Poles endured shortages of just about everything then: meat, gasoline, furniture, chocolate, and in jam-making season, a staple as basic as sugar itself. If communism were to conquer the Sahara, the old joke went, a shortage of sand was destined to follow. Poles stood in long lines to buy just about everything: from such basics as bread or sanitary napkins—boxes of Western tampons, like bottles of Polish vodka, greased the wheels of fortune during the Communist days, the most desired of bribes—to treats such as bananas or lemons, whose occasional appearances, in a country that tends to drink its tea with lemon, always provoked crowds eager to buy. Poles put up with frequent blackouts, hopeless telephones, gritty drinking water, wiretapping of private homes, and general government harassment of its supposed enemies, both local and Western. Even the colors of daily life seemed wrong: tap water was slightly brown, milk was slightly blue, children's faces, except in high summer, were wan.

Once John and I finally got through the chaos of immigration and customs—always fraught during the cold war years— we headed straight to the New York Times house, an oversize, frumpily grand villa built by a well-off railroad engineer in the 1930s, well before the Communist takeover. We set the rosemary and basil plants in the sunniest spot we could find, on the sills of the enormous windows that lined the south side of the living room and overlooked a big, wraparound veranda. Pear, cherry, apple, and apricot trees filled the tiny bit of garden that the Communists had not seized after the war.

It was a Sunday, so attic offices of the *Times* were uncharacteristically silent. The rain, cold and steady, was nothing like the occasional hot summer deluges that Romans pray for, a momentary respite from months of unending heat. It was only August but I was soon rifling my suitcase, looking to see if I had thought to bring a warm sweater on the plane. Both of us started rummaging around the kitchen until we found a canister of tea, and we made a big pot, hoping its heat and warmth would chase away the case of jitters that had settled over us after our footsteps started to echo in that empty house.

The truth was that neither of us was totally prepared for the new life together we had so eagerly awaited. Until the day we arrived in Warsaw, I had seen John cry from happiness, not sadness. Now his mood plummeted when he thought about Peter and Anna back in West Germany with their mother, and the weeks he would have to wait before they could visit us. I watched the tears pour down his cheeks and felt derailed: there was nothing I could do to stop him missing his children. He was fretting too about how long it would take for his Polish to become good enough for him to work on his own, and I was worrying about trading religious news, which I loved, for political news, which had always left me vaguely cold.

That first evening in Warsaw, we pulled ourselves out of our afternoon funk and headed downtown for our first meal together in our new home city. We checked out the restaurants on the main historic square and chose the one that looked most inviting. A pleasant waiter brought over enormous menus, with dozens of possibilities. Jitters at bay, we were eager to begin trying to decipher the menu, offering by offering. After a certain amount of head scratching and consulting of a pocket dictionary, we each decided what we would eat. When the waiter returned to take our order, he responded to each of our requests with the same staccato response: *"Nie ma"*—There isn't any—one of the few Polish phrases I already knew. We were getting our first lesson in Polish-style communism, that restaurant menus were basically a charade—long lists of fantasy meals that the management might have liked to serve had the ingredients been available.

We ended up eating the only dishes the kitchen could provide that rainy Sunday night: clear beet broth with tiny mushroom-filled pierogi (excellent), followed by duck roasted with apples (good, but fatty), and a salad of grated carrot and celery root fixed in a cream dressing (ghastly). It was a meal that filled our stomachs but offered little to our souls, good enough in its own way, but after our Roman experience, certainly unremarkable. We had no idea that we would eat that identical restaurant meal scores of times during our years in Poland; it was as if the Communist bureaucracy had ruled long before that those three dishes, along with the occasional herring or roast pork or turkey breast with canned pineapple, were the only culinary possibilities throughout the land.

No wonder, then, that on the rare occasions when John and I would be in Warsaw at the same time we ate mainly at home or at the home of the same few close friends. Long overseas assignments tend to turn friends into ersatz family. So whenever our jobs weren't pushing us to socialize—at diplomatic dinners and receptions, at private dinners or over drinks with opposition leaders—we relaxed at home with our pretend relatives, a few reporter couples who felt like family. We usually congregated at the Los Angeles Times house, whose resident border collie, Oomba, having no sheep to herd, happily herded us instead. Oomba liked to keep us together, in a huddle around the dining room table, eating, talking, and laughing.

I loved those evenings, when Chuck Powers, the *L.A. Times* reporter, would barbecue us freshly butchered pork loins that he might have found on his last trip to the countryside; when his wife, Cheryl Bentsen, would throw together a salad; when John or I would cook a saffron risotto or spaghetti Bolognese to start the meal; when the Associated Press or *Washington Post* couples would bring some homemade dessert. When we would finish one of those lazy suppers and finally leave the table, Oomba would bark, twitching with worry for our safety, until he had efficiently herded us, his human flock, into a snug corner of the living room.

But our best memories of Warsaw stem from real family visits: when Anna, seven, who attended German schools, learned to count and add in English by playing endless games of Monopoly with Peter, John, and me; when we took the children on a weeklong tour of northern Poland so far from established tourist routes that we bunked in a vacation resort meant for Communist business managers, where a large family of mice noisily gnawed on the sofa stuffing all night long; when John's brother, Paul, brought his family the very week that the Communists were voted out of power.

Both John and I worked flat-out that week in July 1989, trying to capture the sense of history being made, the first Soviet satellite slipping out of its postwar Russian orbit. Each night that Paul, Chan, Drew, and Emily were there, dinner got served later and later, until the night of the election itself, when we didn't even get to the table until long after midnight. That night we ate, and toasted ordinary Poles, who after nearly half a century of oppression had finally bested the Communist usurpers.

Many of our friends in the opposition were accustomed to unemployment, dead-end jobs, jail, and threats against them and their children. Suddenly they were about to become Poland's new leaders: government ministers, ambassadors, newspaper editors, television executives. It was one of those rare, giddily momentous turns of history that provoked emotional goose-flesh, akin to watching Barack Obama sworn in as the first black president of the United States. Long after all of us had left Poland, I realized Oomba's innate need to herd and guard us had been sound. We all needed watching over as the old life began to teeter before the fall.

4 ❧ Chicken

When I was born, and my father's mother learned that I was to be christened Paula, she railed at the heavens and told my parents she would never accept the idea that her first grandchild would carry a name that sounded for all the world to her like *pollo*, the Italian word for chicken.

I never heard this story until I was ten or eleven, when my mother, out of my father's hearing, whispered to me that Angelina had always hated my name. The story rang true: my grandmother never called me anything but Piccinin, which means "little one" in her Venetian dialect. My mother's whisperings also made me realize that my father's curious pet name for me—Chicken—whose history I had never questioned, was not just an idle nickname but his own brand of quiet determination to name his firstborn whatever he and my mother wished. Angelina had been dead for a couple of years before we learned just how determined she had been to christen me Rita.

I was twenty-one and visiting Italy for the first time when I learned from my father's relatives in Verona that they had had no idea who I was when they got my letter saying I was coming to meet them. I understood only the simplest phrases in Italian then, and they spoke no English. To make sure I understood what they were trying to say, they brought out a box of old photos sent from my grandmother over the years. There were snapshots of my baptism, first communion, high school graduation, and numerous photos of me standing near the magnolia tree in my grandparents' front garden. Cousin Marisa turned the photos over so I couldn't help getting the point: each was marked "Rita" in my grandmother's neat hand. Though I found my grandmother's lie little short of monstrous at the time, I have over the years developed a perverse soft spot for the dauntless strength of her will, perhaps because I suspect I inherited a certain useful stubbornness of my own directly from her. In any event, it seems I had always been a different person in Italy than I was in the United States, even before I'd ever been there.

By the autumn of 1989, two years after we had arrived in Warsaw, the lush basil plant that John had carried with us from Rome looked like a couch-ridden invalid. Perched on the broad, south-facing windowsills of our living room, it tried to make the most of the heat from the triple radiators below, but two years of Warsaw's weak northern light and bitter winters had leached its leaves of their heady flavor and vibrant color. Still, the plant hung on against all odds, and we became grudgingly accustomed to its paler northern taste. Italy's pungent flavors were already becoming memories.

The memories that would replace them were nowhere near as pleasant once the Soviet bloc began to come unglued. Mikhail Gorbachev's program of glasnost, or openness, had unlocked doors throughout the Eastern bloc and the Poles were the first to bolt. The East Germans were next, and once the Berlin Wall was breached on November 9, 1989, the rest of the dominoes of Eastern Europe began falling West, too. Czechoslovakia started to topple eight days after the fall of the wall, with a march by university students determined to force out their Communist leaders as the Poles and East Germans before them. Though it began with police violence, the media dubbed it the Velvet Revolution.

It was at this protest that I was beaten, Czechoslovak riot police dragging me and a colleague who had come to my aid, Tyler Marshall of the *Los Angeles Times*, into a dingy building entryway. I don't know how long it went on, though it seemed long. Much of it seemed like a film, being played in slow motion for an audience of one. My head was bleeding the way heads always bleed, copiously, from two large openings where I had been initially clubbed unconscious. Tyler's brand-new Burberry trench coat seemed to have served as a sponge for much of it. My own coat, which looked like a down sleeping bag with sleeves, and which had protected me from many of the body blows, was bloodied as well. My blouse, sweater, and skirt were wet, too, as blood seeped down my neck and dripped south. At some point the cops who were beating us withdrew, and new cops, without riot sticks, appeared and waited until an ambulance arrived. We were put inside with another casualty, a hysterical teenage girl caught up in the violence by chance. Left at a nearby hospital, I was treated by a doctor who shaved narrow portions of my head to clean my two wounds, spritzed them with an anesthetic, sewed me up with what looked and felt like transparent fishing line, then wrapped my filthy head in white gauze.

The doctor filled out a form attesting to the treatment and handed it to me. Well after midnight, long after my deadline, I was allowed to leave the hospital with Iva Drapalova, the retired Associated Press bureau chief, whom Tyler had called to alert. Her coming was an unsought kindness I can never repay. Iva tried to talk me into going home with her rather than returning to my hotel, but I wanted to contact the *Tribune* foreign desk and John, who was in Warsaw, to let them know what had happened. Iva dropped me off at the Alcron, the faded Art Deco hotel where I always stayed in Prague. The desk clerk gasped when she saw me, my head completely swathed in white bandages, my ankle-length down coat still soaked with blood. She let me send my telex to my editors, then with uncharacteristic speed got me a phone line to Warsaw. I didn't want John to hear from news reports or colleagues that I'd been beaten.

When John came on the line, I felt comforted, as I always did, just by the sound of his voice. But when I told him what had happened, his reaction only unnerved me once more. "It's all my fault," he said again and again. I tried to argue that it had had nothing to do with him, but no matter what I said, I could not bring him around. "I brought you here," he kept repeating, his voice full of sorrow. "It's all my fault." Still in shock from the night's events, I hung up the phone thinking that our brief conversation felt like yet another *thwack* of a riot stick.

Slowly climbing the stairs to my room, I realized that John's unexpected response to the beating upset me nearly as much as the beating itself. And it suddenly hit me that no matter how similar our backgrounds had been, our psychological makeups were very different. In times of severe stress, John felt guilty, unlike me, who always got angry. I was angry at the cops who beat me, angry at the Communist apparatus still vainly trying to cling to power. I was angry at myself, for not having gotten out of the situation earlier, in time to file my story; angry that I had missed a deadline for the first time in my career; angry at John for not understanding that his feeling of responsibility for my beating made no psychological sense at all to me. And then, with pitch-perfect bad timing, I realized that our wedding was less than two weeks away. For the first time since we had met four years earlier, I felt a sudden twinge of fear about our future. My anger, his guilt: neither emotion was exactly an ideal thing to bring to our wedding, nor was the idea that our dynamic as a couple seemed subtly changed.

I stayed in Prague another two days, long enough to tell a colleague on the *Tribune*'s foreign desk all that had happened, a rambling conversation that the paper published as a story, and then I flew home to Warsaw. John, who was never good around blood, met me at the airport, looking increasingly green as he took in my bandaged head and my ankle-length parka, both still covered in dried blood. He put his arms around me and held on tight, then took my hand and drove me home. We turned in very early that night, for now it was John's turn to leave for Prague. After he left early the next morning, the headaches began: deep, pounding pains that did not go away for weeks. My face swelled in the coming days, until it was no longer recognizable even to me. My entire face, especially around the eyes, was grotesquely bloated, black and blue. As the days passed, the swelling seemed to shift south, from forehead to under the eyes, to nose, to cheeks. The bruises faded first to purple, then to green, and finally to yellow.

My bruises had already turned to green about a week later, when John and I flew to Rome to clear the final bureaucratic hurdles before our wedding. I told myself that the dynamic between John and me had not essentially changed but only that I understood it better. By the time the flight landed in Rome, both of us had managed to put the beating aside for the time being and we were once again excited at the thought that the wedding we had long been planning was finally about to happen. By the time we took our vows in Rome's ornate wedding hall atop the Capitoline Hill, my bruises had faded to yellow.

Our wedding, perhaps like many second marriages, ended up feeling like a somewhat thrown-together affair, squeezed into a lull in the revolutions spreading throughout Eastern Europe. For the ceremony, I had packed an old dress I loved, but a longtime UPI friend, Cathy Booth, then working for *Time* magazine, insisted I buy something new. Two nights before the ceremony she dragged me through an endless series of shops not far from the Spanish Steps until I found a suit she deemed festive enough for the occasion. She also insisted I carry a bouquet, and silenced my objections by saying she would arrange it all. When the florist failed to appear at her apartment before she left for the ceremony, she threw together a bridal bouquet from flowers she happened to have in a vase in her living room. All the initial photos of the wedding show me carrying Cathy's simple, homemade bouquet. The florist, in typical Roman style, arrived at city hall just as we were called in for the ceremony. His bouquet, stiff and formal, had none of the charm of Cathy's posies, but for a bride who hadn't wanted to carry a bouquet at all, I ended up with two.

John and I had booked a big table at the same restaurant where we had celebrated our departure from Rome two years earlier. Just ordering off the menu, we had a long, delicious meal, full of chatter, good wishes, congratulatory telegrams, and endless happy photos, none of them posed. Only after we finished the main course did I realize that we had completely forgotten to arrange for a wedding cake. I could handle my last-minute purchase of a suit, the mix-up with the flowers, even the chaos of twenty friends trying to order a wedding feast off a menu. But completely forgetting to arrange a wedding cake sent a shiver of misgiving through me. Forgetting the cake seemed unforgivable.

Normally I dismissed Roman *scaramanzia*—all the touching of wood and other gestures that Romans routinely practice to ward off evil—but I found myself touching wood under the tablecloth anyway. The missing cake made me feel that we had somehow failed to keep our wedding feast. Even second marriages deserve a better start than that.

Before the ceremony, I had bought a tube of pancake makeup and covered my face with foundation to erase the traces of my fading bruises. I gamely parted my hair on the wrong side, to hide the scars and bits of surgical thread that were still working their way out of my scalp. Everybody told me I looked fine, and the photos my brother took of John and me show no evidence of the beating, just a radiant bride. We all had a laugh over one of the *Tribune*'s wedding presents: a blue plastic batting helmet from the Chicago Cubs, to keep my head safe for my next revolution. I didn't realize it then, but the *Tribune*'s other present, a small silver clock, was already ticking off the time till the next round.

Given the speed with which the Soviet bloc was falling apart, neither John nor I had wanted to ask our editors for extra time to take a honeymoon, so we flew directly from Rome back to Prague, where Communist leaders were still hanging on to power by a thread. The Czechoslovak secret police lifted our wedding snapshots from our hotel room to let us know they were watching, and we never saw those photos again. By the time the protesters finally managed to push the Communists out—and many of our dissident, jailbird Czechoslovak friends assumed the reins of power—it was nearly Christmas.

We had always intended to take a real honeymoon once the Christmas holidays were over, once our work life calmed down, once Eastern Europe's revolutions had all played out. It was only years later, the trip never taken, that I realized we hadn't missed our honeymoon, but that we had taken it before the ceremony. The two years we had gotten to know each other in Italy as well as the two years we had spent in Poland before our wedding were full of magic and promise, the time when we got to enjoy our very new lives as a couple, even if we were more often physically apart than together. It was the solid bedrock of the joy of those years that saved us both once the troubles began.

5 ❦ Struffoli

*T*he Christmases of my childhood were always two-day feasts: the meatless *vigilia* of Christmas Eve, and the ravioli and roast beef of Christmas Day. One thing was clear: they centered more on the table than under the tree.

On Christmas Eve we kept the traditional Christmas fast in the sense that we ate no meat. But in terms of quantities, it was the Christmas feast we kept. We ate Uncle Joe's cherrystone clams, run quickly under the broiler with garlic, parsley, and a few drops of good olive oil. We ate bowls of spaghettini with clams, cooked briefly with garlic, clam broth, white wine, olive oil, and scads of fresh, flat-leaf parsley and freshly ground black pepper. Sometimes we ate scampi, large shrimp broiled in olive oil, butter, garlic, parsley, and lemon juice until they were just barely beginning to turn pink. The grown-ups would feast on my grandmother Jennie's smoked eel and on her *baccalà*, salt cod, both of which my cousin Paul, brother Danny, and I pretended not to see and tried not to smell. Jennie would produce platters of eggplant and roasted sweet red peppers, bathed in olive oil and garlic slivers.

A huge green salad signaled dessert was on its way: a mountain of Jennie's Neapolitan *struffoli*, cherry-sized balls of sweet, eggy dough, fried till golden, drenched in honey, then covered in walnuts and multicolored sprinkles. As a child I loved prying those sticky, honey-covered fritters apart almost as much as I loved the taste of them, but I always saved the walnut halves for last, all gooey with honey and bristling with sprinkles. To finish off the meal, we opened tiny boxes of lemon- or orange-flavored *torrone*, stark white nougat stuffed with almonds, bought at the Italian grocery at Main and Capitol.

By two p.m. on Christmas Day, we were always back at the table, somehow ravenous again despite what we had consumed the night before. On Christmas we always ate ravioli, large, round pillows of tender, homemade pasta filled with ricotta, Parmigiano, parsley, and eggs. Tiny Nana Gabriel was my cousin Paul's paternal grandmother and no blood relation to us, but my brother and I considered her our third grandmother, not only on the strength of her hand-rolled ravioli and homemade sausages but also on the strength of her patter—a nonstop monologue of jokes, stories, and impersonations of her customers at

Gabriel's Meat Market. Nana Gabe would hover near the two huge pasta pots, murmuring incantations against the possibility that her creations might open and spill their cheesy contents into the bubbling water.

We called them "ravees" and ate them drenched in a tomato *ragù* enriched with every kind of meat imaginable, from meatballs and sausages that Nana Gabe had made herself, to a bit of chicken, some meaty pork ribs, and braciole, thin scallops of tough beef rolled around an herbal stuffing that stewed in the sauce till tender. After we had downed the ravees and the gravy meat, the roast beef would appear, dark and crusty on the outside but bloody rare inside, just the way we all liked it.

After salad, desserts began appearing: roast chestnuts, with rough crosses carved into their tough hides to keep them from exploding on the fire; almonds and walnuts; dried figs and dates; Jennie's famous Swedish butter cookies, the recipe learned decades earlier from a Swedish neighbor; more of Jennie's *struffoli*; more boxes of *torrone*; and finally, for my cousin, brother, and me, candy canes and popcorn balls, the only proof that we were American, and not feasting in a dining room located somewhere in Italy.

John's childhood Christmases were similar to mine, celebrated year after year at the same big mahogany table that now sits with pride of place in a niece's dining room. Even the menus were not all that different. The Tagliabue family ravioli were rectangular and filled with meat, rather than round and filled with ricotta, but John remembers the same big slab of roast beef on the Christmas table in Jersey City that I remember on our table in Connecticut. Although my childhood memories of Christmas are happy, John remembers an undercurrent of sadness in his otherwise upbeat home. His father, Charlie, was sure to weep at some point every holiday. Charlie's father had died decades earlier on an Easter Sunday, and Charlie's mother on the Christmas Eve when John was nearly four. All John's holiday memories struggle to reconcile the joy and the tears the holidays brought forth.

The first bad news of my life arrived by telephone, a cheery yellow model that hung on our cheery yellow kitchen wall. I have never fully trusted phones since. I like my bad news written down, so it can be read silently, so it can be brought to a quiet corner and taken in slowly, at a speed you can stand. When bad news is delivered in a rush of sobs or spoken words that charge into your ear and mind and heart and stomach, when bad news is disembodied from a human face, the badness of the news is magnified many times over. The mind—mine, at least—replays the sobs and the words and the news, over and over, without rest. The replays churn my heart, clutch my stomach, etch deep inside my skull the news I don't want to accept.

I started hating telephones the year I was nine and my brother was two, when a phone conversation I overheard between my mother and hers let me know that he was suddenly dangerously ill. A toddler in yellow pajamas is an unlikely savior, but even at the age of nine I knew Danny had saved me. He kept me from being an only child, took half my mother's heat. Unlike me, he was unfailingly good-natured and kept our mother too busy to brood. His mouth seemed permanently set in a wide grin, and he had the kind of dark-haired, long-lashed beauty so arresting that housewives pushing their carts through the A&P would stop my mother, a stranger, in the aisles to rave. I had pale blue eyes and pale "spaghetti hair," as my grandmother Jennie used to sigh, brushing and brushing it a hundred strokes, hoping it might magically develop Danny's curls, or my mother's rich chestnut color. Nothing seemed fair. Saviors weren't supposed to get sick. Saviors weren't supposed to be in need of saviors themselves.

I came home from school to learn that Danny had developed nephrosis, a kidney ailment that, until the invention of cortisone, used to kill its victims before they were four. He was already lying in a crib in St. Vincent's, the hospital where the nuns wore the same winged headdresses as the nuns at my school, but whose robes were a ghostly white instead of a comforting navy blue. I was not yet sure what it all meant.

My mother, always described in our family as high-strung, was acting higher-strung than I ever remembered her. I knew that high-strung normally meant yells—nervous, angry, howling yells that escaped her throat before she really knew they were lurking inside her head. High-strung meant that when you came in the back door from school, you waited till you rounded the corner from the hallway to the kitchen to see which mother had her hands in the sink. There was the mother who happily asked how school had gone and poured my milk and gave me a couple of my grandmother Jennie's homemade oatmeal cookies. And there was the other mother, always a stranger, who would be standing there quiet and sad or shaking and howling with anger, her hands in dishwater or scrubbing at vegetables, trying to pretend nothing was wrong.

But on this day, she was sobbing and crying without control, a version of high-strung I had never seen, and frightened, I ran up to my bedroom. When I heard her dialing the phone, though, I silently slipped back down to eavesdrop from the front hall. Talking to Jennie, she sobbed more than talked. It took only a few minutes to realize that the brother for whom I had waited seven years might not come back home. She mentioned cortisone, a new drug then, which the doctors hoped might keep the disease in check, but even then they were concerned about its possible long-term effects.

Twenty-four days after our wedding in Rome, I was downstairs in the Times house in Warsaw when I heard the telex machine in John's attic office clatter to life. It was shortly after two p.m. on Christmas Eve. I was hoping it was John, finally cabling to tell me he had arrived in Romania, where he had been sent to report.

It was to have been our first Christmas and New Year's together as newlyweds. We had had a full, happy holiday planned: an old friend was flying in from Rome, we were hosting Christmas Eve dinner with our closest Warsaw friends, and Peter and Anna were coming for the week after New Year's. Then, the week before Christmas, the Romanians toppled Nicolae Ceaușescu, the most hated Communist dictator in the Eastern bloc. John was on his way to cover the heavy fighting, our personal plans abruptly overturned.

Ordinarily I would have gone to report, too, but five weeks after my beating, my wounds still felt fresh, my scars still hairless slashes, fish-belly white, across my scalp. I was still having severe headaches and felt drained after so little as climbing a flight of stairs. Most of all, I felt a strong premonition of danger.

Uncharacteristically panicky, I had cried and argued with John to refuse the Romania assignment, even though rationally I knew he couldn't possibly beg off the story. Finally, I talked myself into believing that my premonition was nothing more than fallout from my beating. I heard myself agree that while he was gone I would try to salvage Christmas with the help of Cathy, our *Time* magazine friend from Rome who was already en route to Warsaw. John promised to do his best to return in time for Peter and Anna's visit.

The next day, the noisy rattle of the telex machine sent me

running up the two flights of stairs to John's office. The telex was not, as I had been praying, from John but from my foreign desk at the *Tribune*. It was eerily short, with a peculiar demand: I was to call immediately one of the *Tribune*'s main editors, the man who had hired me, at his home outside Chicago. When I finally managed to get through, I was told what I had begun to fear: John had been shot.

Cathy and I spent the rest of Christmas Eve trying to sift through utterly conflicting reports about details of John's shooting the previous night. The only solid information available was that he had been shot while riding in a car in Timişoara, the city where the revolution had erupted, and that the colleagues with whom he was traveling had left him in a municipal hospital before continuing on to the capital, Bucharest.

At some point I called the Los Angeles Times house to tell them the news, only to receive a second shock: One of our closest friends in Warsaw, John Daniszewski of the Associated Press, also had been wounded the previous night. Incredibly, he too had been shot in an unrelated attack in Timişoara the same night as my John, though neither of them knew the other was even there, much less lying wounded in different hospitals.

Later that evening, the remnants of our Christmas Eve dinner party gathered as planned: John Daniszewski's wife, Drusie; Cheryl Bentsen, whose husband, Chuck, was trying to get into

Romania for the *L.A. Times*; our house guest, Cathy; and me. Each of us was doing what came naturally: Cathy was drinking; Cheryl was smoking; Drusie was popping Christmas cookies; and I was in the kitchen, preparing the crabmeat risotto I had been planning to serve before news of the shootings had reached us. None of us was hungry, no one particularly wanted to eat. But I was hoping that the habitual motions of chopping onions and stirring rice would remind me of normality, make me feel less crazed, make both Johns somehow miraculously unhurt. It didn't work.

I have a single photo of that Christmas Eve taken in our living room. The tree is standing in the background. Plates of Christmas cookies and cakes, baked before the news came in, are resting on a table in the foreground. Cheryl, chin in hand, is sitting in an armchair, staring off at nothing. "Christmas in hell," I later wrote on its back, though we had not quite reached our destination yet.

Christmas morning, twelve hours after learning both Johns had been shot, Drusie and I set off to join them. Christmas dinner was the ham and Snickers special of the Polish airline. Christmas supper was take-out Chinese in Paris, of all places, where after a day of airline hell Drusie and I ended up, twice as far away from our wounded husbands as when we had started out that fogbound morning in Warsaw. Chopsticks in hand, we sat around the table of one of my John's colleagues, who with his wife and two children helped us get through the surreal nightmare of that holiday evening. I was trying to talk myself into believing that John wasn't badly injured, or that he might be evacuated to Yugoslavia by the time I finally got there. Deep down, I didn't believe it for a minute.

6 ❧ Potions

When I was seven or eight and still prone to occasional childhood fevers, I craved a cup of my mother's sickroom tea. Nothing tasted better, when I had a 101-degree fever, than hot tea, not too strong, sweetened with honey and floating a thin wedge of lemon, served in one of my mother's special china cups. The trick was to drink it at just the right speed, not so slowly that the tea began to cool, not so fast that the lemon failed to mellow in the hot, golden liquid. When the tea was finished, the lemon lay at the bottom of the cup, and I would gnaw the pulp away from the rind and imagine the fever germs withering away. Whenever I needed my mother's sickroom tea, my mother and I would observe an undeclared truce: mother stopped barking, daughter stopped sassing. I almost always recovered by morning.

If the fever was higher—102, 103, or accompanied by flu or measles or stomach woes—the potion was ginger ale, cool and bubbly, a single ice cube bobbing in a highball glass. Once the fever dropped, my mother brought dry toast, too; hot, golden, and sliced into four triangles—never the two coarse rectangles of workaday toast—in an effort to appeal to my lost appetite.

As the illness began to wane, stronger potions would appear: Angelina's homemade chicken broth, made from one of the oldest hens that pecked in the stinky coop in the back corner of their garden. I loved my grandmother's chicken soup and the chicken feathers she stuffed into our pillows almost as much as I hated the chickens themselves and the acrid ammonia stench of their dark, airless henhouse. If my stomach was still weak, then the broth came plain, or with a bit of minced parsley added at the last minute. If I was feeling stronger, then it appeared with soft shreds of white meat and tiny, star-shaped pastina.

When I got to the jammed surgical ward at Spital 2, the hospital in Timişoara where John had been lying for five days, going in and out of consciousness, I was struck as much by the hunk of heavy brown bread and the thick, gristly pork sausage—both untouched at the head of his bed—as by John's gray, skeletal face. No dainty toast triangles here. No honey-flavored, lemon-laced tea. No fancy medical machinery. No antibiotics. Not even enough bandages. Just a sudden flood of patients, some moaning, some ominously quiet. And a truce of sorts. The fighting that had raged around the hospital a few nights earlier, as Ceaușescu's security forces battled army regulars and the people of Timișoara, had stopped.

In my halfhearted attempt to stave off panic, I had tried to believe that the conflicting reports on the nature and serious-ness of John's wounds were overdramatized. But when the ele-vator doors at Spital 2 opened to reveal a huge gob of spit on the filthy floor, I no longer needed to see John's eyes—wild and unnaturally bright in the gray, drawn face of a suddenly elderly stranger—to know that most of the condition reports that had filtered back to me had been hopelessly optimistic. He looked like a desiccated caricature of the man I had kissed good-bye at Frankfurt Airport five days earlier.

John was conscious, and relief flooded through his eyes when he recognized me, but he was also off his head, lapsing intermit-tently into incoherence from the infection already raging inside him. A nurse was dressing him in what was left of his shot-up clothes, and he was lying on an old-fashioned metal bed, his hands clenched, clearly desperate to be gone. He kept trying to apologize for having been shot. I took his hands in mine and held them tightly. I was hypnotized by the glittery, ghostly look in his eyes. Those eyes, in which I could see John present one instant, then gone the next, so terrified me that I could almost feel myself disappearing under their gaze. All real feeling—my terror, panic, exhaustion—was being sucked somewhere deep inside me. Holding John's hands, held by his eyes, I felt as if a heavy shroud were slipping over my emotions and feelings, and I was shocked to hear myself suddenly speaking calmly, telling John to hang on, that after days of begging, a German Red Cross plane was waiting at the airport to fly him to safety.

Our trip from hospital to airfield was short, surreal. The orderlies brought John downstairs, literally folding him into the elevator, then folding him again into a filthy station wagon so small that they had to bend him at the knees, because at six-feet-two he was too tall to fit. I sat in front, next to a grizzled driver who was wearing a fezlike hat and stiff woolen coat and taking deep drags on a reeking Eastern bloc cigarette. John lay on his stomach directly behind the driver next to a short, filthy soldier in a World War I–style helmet and heavy greatcoat, smoking, too. The car was narrow as well as short and the silent soldier stood his AK-47 upright, the rifle barrel jammed against John's cheek for the entire ride. John kept thinking it was most likely the same kind of gun that had shot him; I kept checking my purse, obsessively, to make sure I still had John's hospital report, which the doctors in Munich said would be crucial.

Throughout the ride to the airport, John drifted in and out of consciousness. Awake, he talked incessantly, telling me how he remembered riding into Timişoara in darkness, sitting in the front seat of a red Peugeot with a French photographer at the wheel and two other American reporters in back. He remembered a sudden thud against his car door, the door pressing sharply against him, the car suddenly rocking, and the sensation of something small traveling through him, not hurting, just hurtling through. He remembered only one shot, or a single burst of shots, even though the others told him later that the car had been virtually demolished by the fusillade. He remembered losing consciousness, then reawakening as soldiers pulled him from the car, laid him on a stretcher, and raced him into a hospital operating room, where doctors frantically ripped his shirt and undershirt up the back to get at his wound. John was talking as we approached the airport, but fell silent as I looked for our promised transport out.

We seemed to leave Romania the instant we drove around a corner of the empty airport terminal and saw, finally, the Red Cross plane, white and pristine, waiting on the empty tarmac, while snowflakes began to drift down. In truth, it took a long time to get off the ground, as we had to wait, while John's thin canvas stretcher lay on the bitterly cold tarmac, for a beefy border guard to rubber-stamp our passports, and for the Germans to be satisfied with our paperwork, which they checked and rechecked before allowing us to board.

The antiseptic cleanliness of the little Learjet, whose interior had been fitted out as a state-of-the-art emergency room, made the Romanian hospital look like a medieval charnel house. A Red Cross doctor and nurse were already pulling off John's parka and attaching him to various intravenous tubes as I climbed aboard and we took off. Once the doctor completed her initial tests, she radioed her findings directly to Munich's Klinikum Rechts der Isar, so that emergency room doctors would be ready to act when we arrived. The doctor in charge looked grave when he saw us, five days—nearly 120 hours—after the shooting.

A crowd of emergency room doctors and nurses materialized, swarming around John and rolling him away. Just before the big double doors swung shut, the last of the doctors turned to me. I looked at him, hoping he might be able to calm my rising fear. Instead, he began to berate me for taking so long to get John to Munich. Stung by his curt tone and the implication that I had purposely kept John hospitalized in Romania as long as possible for some unimaginable reason, I felt like a child again, when my mother, on one of her bad days, accused me of committing an absurd, imaginary crime. There was nothing to be said in either case. But the doctor's last words kept echoing in my brain, causing my stomach to spasm: "Another six to twelve hours and there would have been absolutely nothing we could have done to save him."

I stared at the doctor's back as he turned and walked through the same double doors through which John had disappeared. Suddenly I was alone again, in a nondescript hospital waiting room, my heart pounding noisily and my breath coming in short, irregular bursts. To calm myself, I pulled out the translation of the hastily written, error-filled Romanian medical report that the Germans had requested, reading and rereading it:

Brought in by a citizen from street. Diagnosis: Gunshot wound to lumbar region, with crushing of muscles of the sacro-lumbar region. Pelvic bone fractured in many pieces because bullet exploded there 2–3 vertebrae in lumbar region slightly broken from explosion of bullet.

Done: Dead muscle removed. Little bone fragments removed. Big bullet, not a normal bullet but an explosive bullet. Bullet passed through body. Post-op: Normal for type of bullet and wound.

In intensive care: Gave him blood, intravenous substitution, mineral substitution, acid and basic substitution, anti-tetanus. Cephalosporin, Betalactamin, Metronidazole. Gentamicin (the latter causes liver damage).

Now: Leaving clinic in satisfactory condition with a slight fever. Needs assistance for infection risk and most important because of bone lesions. Liver and kidneys— some trouble because of infections and drugs used. Halothane, an anesthetic, causes liver problems. No signs of paralysis and no reasons to suspect start of same.

I focused, of course, on one line of that report. "Now: Leaving clinic in satisfactory condition with a slight fever." I must have read that line a hundred times as I tried to quell the rising panic I felt each time I pictured John's eyes, glittering in that unearthly way on the ward in Timișoara's Spital 2, glittering so oddly on the Red Cross plane as we took off from Romania into the gathering snowstorm. I read it again and tried to understand it in light of the German doctor's decidedly different diagnosis.

After a few more readings I understood that the single line in the report upon which I had focused was utter rubbish, written to cover the Romanian government in the very likely event of John's death. Chief surgeon Petru Radulescu made that clear during a visit John made to Timişoara eight years later. The only reason the government had opened its airspace to the German Red Cross plane was to get John out while he was still breathing, Dr. Radulescu told him. The government did not want to be in the position of having to ship the dead body of a *New York Times* reporter back to the United States. The references to antibiotics were pure fiction, a wish list of drugs the Romanian doctors coveted, just like those huge Polish restaurant menus we knew so well, the ones that listed dozens of dishes but whose kitchens never had much more to offer than beet soup and roast duck. During their emotional meeting eight years after Ceauşescu's execution, Dr. Radulescu told John that the hospital had absolutely no modern antibiotics at the time of the revolution. "We knew what they were but we didn't have any," he said.

*B*etween the evening of December 23, when he was shot, and December 28, the day he was airlifted to Munich, John underwent three emergency surgeries, two of them in Romania. The Munich surgeons, like the Romanians, tried to clean the large, infected wound of dead tissue. A small piece from the tip of one of his vertebrae had come apart during the procedures, but posed no neurological danger. The initial lab tests, X-rays, and computer scans indicated that John's liver and kidneys would revive once the infection was controlled. We awaited the results of the pathology report to know the exact nature of the infection. But the idea that things could still go horribly wrong once we had made it to the West had not yet sunk in. Even so, that night while John slept, closely monitored in the ICU, I lay awake, my mind working and reworking the last words I heard from the surgeon: "I think we can handle the probable infection."

Six days after the shooting, on December 29, John was still in intensive care. By late morning, his condition had worsened considerably and my mind began to shut down. Exhausted with worry, I realized at some point that I could no longer take in what the doctors were telling me. I tried to compensate by taking copious notes: "It is a large and very infected wound," I wrote. "We removed bone splinters, dead tissue, muscle, and much of the infected material." The doctors foresaw intensive care to heal the wound, a fourth operation the following day to remove additional dead tissue, and weeks of hospitalization.

Despite that report, I did not expect to be so utterly shocked upon seeing the gaunt figure that lay on the hospital bed in the ICU. It was not just the mass of tubes and wires protruding from John's inert body that so disturbed me. It was the sensation of seeing what looked like a corpse—thin-lipped, gray, emaciated, facial features caved in. My eyes and heart saw a shell of a body, lying where I had hoped to see some remnant of the vigorous man I had married twenty-nine days earlier. As I approached John's bed, I had the strongest sensation of having been somehow catapulted forward in time. I felt like an aged widow, come to say good-bye to her even more aged husband, lying dead on his funeral bier.

John was unconscious, and would remain that way for several days. But something, probably terror, propelled me to start talking to him. Trying to sound normal, I said hello, told him he was not looking too peppy, that he needed to rest and regroup and, most of all, to hang on. I reminded him that he was out of Timişoara, that no one was shooting in Munich. I reminded him that he was in one of the best trauma hospitals in Germany and that the doctors were doing everything they could to clean his wound and fight the infection. I talked about Peter and Anna, fourteen and eight, just a few hours' train ride away, and how I would make sure they learned immediately that he was finally in the safety of a good hospital. I talked about his brothers, Charles and Robert and Paul, how they were calling and sending faxes every few hours. I talked about our sisters-in-law, Arlene and Chan. I talked about our nieces and nephews. I talked about my parents, my brother, our friends, our staff in Warsaw, our editors in the States, our colleagues. I talked slowly and softly, but incessantly, for what seemed like forever, trying all the while to sound as normal as I could, not only for him but for myself as well. Though the quiet drone of my voice had no visible effect on John, it helped calm me.

7 🦉 Lentils and Sugar

When I was a child I was fascinated by feasting food, the dishes that different communities or cultures traditionally serve on special occasions. A Greek-British family who lived above us for a couple of years ate a very eggy, flat yellow cake at Eastertide. It tasted wonderful but—even better, from my eight-year-old eyes—contained a dime carefully wrapped in folds of waxed paper. Just as the *fève* in a French *galette des rois* brings a crown at Epiphany, the coin in the Greek cake brought luck to the person in whose slice it was hidden.

New Year's celebrations in Italy always contain lentils, for the consuming of *lenticchie* at this time of year is meant to bring good luck and as many coins as lentils consumed. A similar tradition holds in Texas and much of the American South, where black-eyed peas are eaten at New Year's for health and wealth in the coming year. It is no surprise that both lentils and black-eyed peas cost next to nothing, spreading the possibility of good luck to any family, no matter the purse.

When I was very small I liked the idea of lentils and luck more than the actual eating of them. But I can still see my mother's father, Tony, a short, rounded man who never lost his appetite or his dark hair despite his ninety-plus years, slowly chewing his way through bowl after bowl of them, always flecked with bits of onion, carrot, celery, tomato, and pancetta, a specially cured cut of pork similar to bacon.

As I got older, I looked forward as much to the lentils as the luck. By the time I reached my teens, I also loved the plump, dark pink sausage, *cotechino*, meant to go with them. The best *cotechino*—whose name comes from the Italian word for pork rind, *cotica*, an essential ingredient—is somehow nearly creamy but toothsome at the same time, with a delicate taste and gelatinous broth that one mixes into the lentils. When I moved to Dallas in my late twenties, I happily traded my lentils for Texans' black-eyed peas at New Year's. In the five years I lived there, the lentil–black-eyed pea connection was the only culinary similarity I ever saw between Eye-talian and Texas kitchens.

I ate no lentils at New Year's in Munich. I only thought about it years later, when John and I were back living in Rome. It's not that I think a bowl of lentils would have made any difference, but since then I have never missed a meal of them as each new year rolls round.

A week to the day after John was shot, he underwent a fourth operation to clean out his wound. But the surgery did not go according to plan. John's lungs, like all of his major organs, were suffering from the infection raging within. When his lungs began filling with fluid, the doctors had to pump them out to save him from drowning. After long hours of waiting for news, I was initially relieved to see one of John's surgeons appear, but when he briefed me on what had happened and warned me that John might need to go on a ventilator the next day, my gut ignored his calm delivery, my brain began flirting with panic. That the doctor forbade me to visit John underscored the gravity of the situation. That the doctors had to pump out his lungs to keep him breathing terrified me. That he was going to need yet another operation in forty-eight hours— his fifth since the shooting—sounded ominous. That he might need to go on a breathing machine was a possibility I had never once entertained.

I tried to shut down the whirring in my head and went back to the hotel to find Adele Riepe, the Bonn bureau manager of *The New York Times*, who had spent most of the previous week hammering Red Cross officials in several countries to attempt to evacuate John from Romania. Adele, a former Ford Agency model who in her seventies looks better than I ever did at thirty, took one look at my gaunt face and said she was going to feed me.

We went to a small restaurant just down the street from the hotel and downed a glass of dry white *Frankenwein* while we waited for our food to arrive. I didn't feel hungry, but she pushed me to eat: starter, main course, salad, dessert. *Der Appetit kommt beim Essen*, the Germans say, and they are right. Eating can in fact bring on one's appetite. We emptied every plate the waiter brought, then hurried back to the hotel so that I could call the doctors before turning in.

Most of the news was not good, and it continued to worsen over the New Year's holiday. John's lungs were failing; the infection, which the doctors were now calling septicemia, was still raging; and he was breathing only because he was on a respirator and a pair of lung pumps. He underwent a fifth operation to remove all the tissue that had blackened and died since the previous surgery. The sole encouraging sign was that the lab reports showed that the infection was coming from the wound alone; all nearby organs were untouched. During this period, John would fall into and out of half-conscious dream states that had begun in the hospital in Timişoara and persisted long after he had left the intensive-care unit in Munich. Whether asleep or semiconscious, he kept dreaming he saw a gearbox filled with brightly colored plastic gears turning in various directions and clicking, constantly clicking. John knew, even in his sleep, that if those gears stopped, he would be dead.

*E*ight days after arriving in Munich, the trauma team finally cleared John to leave intensive care for transfer to the hospital's special surgical ward, where they envisioned a three-week course of specialized treatment using something called *Wundzucker*. If all went well, the treatment would be followed by plastic surgery to close the wound.

Neither of us knew the word *Wundzucker*, literally "wound sugar," but a few days later, John noticed what looked like sandy crumbs in his sheets, as if he had been eating cookies in bed. It was only then that he realized that the white crystals the doctors had been pouring into his back twice a day were nothing more than sterilized sugar, administered after he had been bathed in a diluted chamomile extract, and his wound had been hosed out. The hosing produced pain fierce enough to require a morphine chaser.

Sugar, a treatment from Egyptian antiquity, helps heal dangerously infected wounds by killing the powerful bacteria that thrive in their depths, without causing trauma to the surrounding tissue. The practice largely fell out of favor during the 1900s, as pharmaceutical companies developed increasingly powerful antibiotics to fight infection. But in the mid-1980s, German doctors turned back to sugar when they began encountering super-powerful bacteria harbored in deep wounds that did not respond to even the most high-tech preparations. Although U.S. medical experts largely discredit the idea as quaint, European doctors who have readopted the technique say that even dirty wounds often turn free of bacteria after only several days of treatment and that the injuries tend to heal more completely and gently than with standard antibiotics.

Dry sugar crystals have an osmotic effect, drawing the liquid out of all the bacteria that lurk deep inside the wound. The removal of that liquid kills the bacteria that fuel infection. The treatment allows new flesh—the doctors call it "granulation tissue"—to grow deep inside the wound, which, in John's case, was exactly what was needed. His wound was so large and deep that it could not just be closed; there was no flesh in the trench with which to close it. Instead it had to heal slowly, from the bottom up, and it did, over a period of weeks.

John's doctors always worried that the infection would spread into his shattered pelvic bone, a situation they wished to avoid. Bone infections were nasty, they said, horrifically painful for the patient and tricky to heal. Although they would have liked to wait until enough new flesh formed to simply close the wound, the risk of infection was too great. They would give the granulated sugar three weeks' time to begin producing a base of granulation tissue. Then they would call in the plastic surgeons, to finish off the job more quickly.

On the first day of the sugar treatment, I arrived to find the surgical ward's second-in-command already studying his new patient's wound while changing John's bandages. I had never actually seen the wound, and when the doctor began to say how much better it looked, and asked if I wanted to have a look, too, I naively nodded.

Clearly I had been keeping the gory details of John's injury in some sort of psychological safe house, for when I stepped up to John's bedside to look, I felt as if I were staring into an abyss so deep that I was afraid I would fall in. For some time I had known intellectually that John's wound was large and had to have been made larger by the five operations in which the doctors had cut away dead flesh. But I was not at all prepared to see a horizontal trench wider than my forearm stretching from one side of his waist to the other, his spinal column looking like a white bridge over the dark red meat of his open back. It looked for all the world as if someone had taken an ice cream scoop and roughly carved a deep trench across his middle.

I am not particularly squeamish, but the wound so unnerved me that I had to turn away. The doctor noticed my distress and began talking softly, describing how much better the wound looked now, noting that the dark pink-red color was a sign of solid granulation, and pointing out that there was no longer any dead, black flesh. After he finished rebandaging the wound, we walked out of the room together into the hallway.

As soon as the heavy door to John's room closed, the doctor apologized, saying he had assumed I'd seen the wound while John was in intensive care. Still reeling, I demanded to know if there was any hope at all of a wound that size actually healing. "Don't worry," he said. "We close bigger holes than that."

That night, when I went back to my hotel room, all the fear and panic I had been suppressing for the previous two weeks let loose. I sobbed, unable to catch my breath, for what seemed like hours before I calmed down enough to check with another expert on battlefield wounds.

My father had spent years in the South Pacific during World War II, and was assigned to an army medical unit, where he ferried the wounded and the dead from the battlefield to field hospitals. My mother had told me when I was a child that he did not like to talk about the war. His only sporadic comments about it usually erupted in response to newspaper stories quoting members of Veterans of Foreign War societies. Anybody who would join a group like that, he would say, must have spent the entire war in a cushy office on a U.S. base. His premise was that nobody who actually saw fighting would ever want anything further to do with the military. The only time he willingly discussed his five-year stint was the night he and I went to see M*A*S*H at a local movie house. He loved it, the first war movie he had ever seen that caught the crazed reality of war.

I dialed home and tried to describe for my father the size and depth of the trench across John's back. I told him that the doctor had assured me that healing was possible, but that I wasn't sure if I could believe him. My father was quiet while he searched through the wartime memories he generally kept at bay. "I remember a guy we brought in without a calf," he said. "His calf had basically been blown off. There was pretty much nothing there but bone. I can tell you that the meat grew back. It's amazing what a body can do when it wants to live."

We said good night. I hung on to his words and actually slept.

I used to think that my family's central dynamic may have gotten stuck on food because of the onset of my brother's renal problems when he was two, that my parents never stopped trying to devise a diet that might make his kidneys behave. But in searching through old scrapbooks and notebooks, I found that food was at the center of things long before he got sick. I could not spell "cereal" or "carrots" when Danny took his first solid food at seven weeks, but I was interested enough to write about it on a thin piece of brown construction paper stuck into my first scrapbook. "When my brother was 7 weeks old we gave him cirel," I wrote. "On June 18, my baby brother aet ate carrets he took all that my mother gave him! . . . on June 21 my brother ate Squash."

Nobody remembers if it was Danny's pediatrician who suggested that my parents ensure that he ate a protein-rich diet, to make up for the protein spilling out into his urine, upsetting the body's delicate balances and threatening his life. It is possible that it was something my parents did on their own. But I know that for a dozen years at least, our family's chief work at mealtime was to get my brother to eat plenty of protein-rich foods:

meat, eggs, and dairy products. Like a Greek chorus, my father, mother, and I repeatedly interrupted the chatter of all our meals with a basic line: "Eat your meaty, Danny, eat your meaty."

How familiar and oddly comforting, then, when John got out of intensive care and found himself constantly hungry. The hospital's surgical chief said it was the strongest sign to date that his body was beginning to heal. He also told us that a body successfully growing new flesh would demand a high-protein, high-calorie diet. The hospital would provide it; John was expected to eat it.

From that moment forward, each of John's three daily meals arrived laden with protein-rich foods. Thick slices of cold cuts, large wedges of cheese, hard-boiled eggs, huge chunks of meat or fish, containers of yogurt or milk-rich puddings, whole-grain breads—John's food tray would have made a cardiologist blanch. Consumption of this food was no chore for John; he was ravenous at each mealtime and ate with gusto, from the slabs of liverwurst on thick brown bread to the mounds of herring in sour cream. The granulation of new flesh in his wound was gobbling up the calories and proteins faster than even John could keep pace with, pulling extra protein wherever it could find it. No matter how much he ate, it wasn't enough. John's hair turned brittle in the coming weeks and thinned out dramatically, as the healing wound pulled proteins from even the hair on his head.

He was not the only one with an appetite. I had always had a fast metabolism, and the adrenaline rush from the shock of the shooting and all that followed had only made it faster. Every morning I would go down to the hotel's breakfast buffet and eat dinner-sized portions of scrambled eggs, tiny, herb-flavored sausages known as *Nürnberger Würstchen*, a mound of German-style home fries, crunchy breakfast rolls, yogurt, and bowls of out-of-season berries flown in from someplace south of the equator. Only after I had eaten like this every morning and downed a large pot of tea did I feel physically and mentally ready to return to the hospital.

At lunchtime I would return to the hotel café and eat the daily special—soup, main course, salad, dessert—before I could even think about heading back to the hospital. I would stay with John till after his supper, then eat yet another large meal before falling asleep. No matter how much I ate during those weeks in Munich, my clothes let me know that I was losing weight. My entire body felt stuck in overdrive. Each night I would fall asleep exhausted, but would often awaken with a start just a couple of hours later. I would be breathing hard and in a sweat, as if I had been chased by demons during my sleep. In Munich I never remembered my dreams, but I awoke knowing they had been bad.

John's appetite and protein-rich diet worked as the doctors had hoped, and by the end of January, they were ready to try a pair of operations to finally close up his back. Both went nearly according to plan. The hospital's top cosmetic surgeon basically butterflied John's buttocks, cutting flaps that he could then open out over the wound to patch what remained of the trench. Two weeks later, when I finally saw the wound for the second time, it looked as if a very neat, careful madman had carved his way around it. But to me it was beautiful: the gaping trench and open view of John's spine miraculously gone, replaced by a couple of feet of delicately traced seams. No Frankenstein cross-stitches, just a subcutaneous blind stitch that left neat, clean lines. My nightmares paused.

8 ❧ Birthday Cake

Until I went away to college, my parents, my brother, and I ate virtually every Sunday lunch of my life with a dozen or more of my mother's relatives in my grandparents' tiny apartment. Except for those first moments of silence when everyone dug into the steaming plates before them, Comparato, Romano, Tozzi, Delia, Fucci, and Gabriel never stopped talking, kidding, joking, telling stories, swapping news, or listening to the latest tales of wacky customers at Gabriel's Meat Market. We ate a ritual menu: Jennie's *pasta al ragù*, and then meatballs, sausage, chicken, pork, and braciole, thin slices of herbed, rolled beef, all of which had flavored her thick Neapolitan sauce. A mixed salad, "good for the digestion," always followed the meat.

The only variable dish was dessert, usually one of Jennie's

homemade American specialties: fresh blueberry, apple, cherry, or pumpkin pie, depending on the season; Boston cream or lemon meringue pies on occasion; pineapple crush cake (made with zwieback, eggs, condensed milk, pineapple, and whipped cream); or, on birthdays, my favorite, Auntie's chocolate cake, a moist, sour-milk, two-layer concoction spread thickly with Jennie's soft, white frosting and covered in grated coconut. As a child I loved to watch the vinegar—Heinz's white, not my grandfather's red—start to sour the warm milk. If I stared long enough I could see the milk begin to thicken and coagulate from the chemical reaction with the vinegar. When the cake was pulled from the oven, leaving moist, dark crumbs on the toothpick tester, I loved the sight of it sitting on a cake plate in the center of any of the tables from my childhood, whether it was my birthday or somebody else's.

Jennie and Tony, Great-Uncle Pete, Great-Aunt Philly, Deedee, Auntie and Uncle, Cousin Jo, Cousin Al, my mother: all are gone today, along with all the other great-aunts and great-uncles, and nearly all the second and third cousins who used to join us on special occasions. My grandparents' generation produced few children, my parents' generation even fewer. Aside from me, the only ones left from that great crowd of family that used to celebrate Sundays and birthdays together are my father and brother, and Auntie's son, my lone first cousin, Paul.

I never lost the recipe for Auntie's birthday cake, no matter how many times I have moved. The recipe, stained with melted chocolate and vanilla, travels with me to each new country, each new kitchen. I make Auntie's cake at least once a year. A single bite of that cake still conjures up the days when all the characters of my childhood used to sit around Jennie's kitchen table on Whitney Avenue celebrating the joy of birth, when I was little, when my parents were young, when my grandparents were still only in their sixties. It keeps those Sunday dinners alive in my memory, keeps alive my family dead.

*B*efore John was discharged from the hospital in Munich, a gray-haired orderly named Werner walked into John's room, read his medical chart, and pointedly asked him when he was born. When John responded, Werner—who had acquired a certain wisdom about traumatic wounds while working aboard a hospital ship off the coast of Vietnam—shook his head to disagree. "You've got a new birthday now," he said gently, referring to the date of John's shooting. "December twenty-third, nineteen eighty-nine. It's a new birthday for your new life."

John and I both understood that Werner was not just chatting idly, though at the time we caught but a whiff of what he was trying to convey. It took us a good fifteen years to understand the simple truth he was hinting at, and will probably take years more before we truly, utterly accept it: that the arc of a single bullet finding its mark was not just a shocking, passing incident in our lives but a life-changing one that would make us dramatically different people. Because that single bullet so thoroughly changed John and me, it changed the lives of the children as well, and it will in turn change the lives of any children they have one day, as the memory of that bullet drifts in a slow-moving spiral down the generations. That spiral drifted up the generations, too: my mother never quite got over the shock of John's shooting, the fear that her new son-in-law might die before she got to meet him.

A single bullet started it all. A single bullet fired by a roadside sniper in a nondescript city suddenly convulsed by revolution. Just one bullet found John that night, a bullet that pierced the passenger door of a little red Peugeot before tearing into John's right side and exiting through his left.

But even a single bullet takes at least two paths: one through a body, the other through life itself. The first path is visible, gory, dramatic. All the same, it is the simple route. The second path is imperceptible, hidden, and therefore far more fraught. The second path cuts through a once seamless life, splitting it in two: the old life before the bullet and the new life after. Neither doctors nor patient can see the second path, so the wounds it leaves often go unnoticed and untreated. Both can lead to long-term festering.

That gentle German orderly tried his best to alert us to the bullet's second path, but we were too naive to comprehend. We tried, for several years in fact, to celebrate John's new birthday as if we understood its importance. A year to the day after the shooting, we invited a few close friends to share a "new birthday" dinner with us, to celebrate the fact that John was alive. That I chose not to make Auntie's chocolate cake for the occasion is proof that I still hadn't digested the import of Werner's message. I made a pie that night for dessert, pumpkin, I think. I even stuck a single, lighted birthday candle in the middle of it, but all of us at the table felt awkward and off-stride. No one felt comfortable "celebrating" John's new birthday, because accepting a new birthday meant accepting a new person. Accepting the new John meant the old John was gone, a concept none of us was ready to acknowledge.

In the nearly twenty years that have passed since that phony birthday party, one thought continues to haunt: If a single bullet travels up and down the generations, how do we ever begin to measure the havoc of war?

Shortly after Werner's birthday speech, old friends from Rome who had moved to a dune-filled stretch of white beach on Key Biscayne called to urge us to take a total break once John was released from the Munich hospital and had completed his rehabilitation at a Connecticut clinic. They invited us to spend a week with them in the Florida sunshine, where both of us could escape the medical world, which had become our daily grind. It was our first taste of the role that friends, sunshine, food, talk, and laughter would later play in John's recovery, though we hadn't yet the ghost of an idea about how far off that recovery actually was.

It took little time to be seduced by Don and Marybelle Schanche's idea of sunshine, sea air, stone crabs, and Key lime pie. The mere idea of it was the carrot that kept us going during the rest of John's hospital care. I can still feel that welcoming blast of Florida's enveloping heat and humidity as we stepped off the plane in Miami, pure bliss after months in the gray, damp cold of a northern European winter.

An hour later we were inside our friends' light-filled apartment, and the only thing between their terrace and the bright, shining sea was an enormous, heated swimming pool surrounded by sea grape, grass, and the occasional lizard tumbling out of a palm tree. The sun beat down, heating our bones, unknotting our muscles, even beginning to dispel our panic.

Their apartment was filled with reminders of our shared time in Italy, from the gaily painted Italian pottery they had collected over the years to the framed sketches of Rome hanging on the walls, to the lazy evening meals that Marybelle served us, just as she had served us in Rome. Perhaps as much as anything that reminded me of Rome was the fierce, bright sunlight of early spring in Key Biscayne, which had the power to banish from my memory the weak winter light of northern Europe.

I remember sitting close to John and drinking in the intensity of that sunlight while sipping a glass of cold, very cold, white wine, not unlike the bottles we used to share on our sunny, plant-filled terraces in Rome. Don had a booming, infectious laugh; Marybelle, a higher, full-throated chortle, like the exultant pealing of a high-toned bell. Between the sunshine, the wine, and their laughter, I felt as if I had somehow gotten out of hell and peeked into heaven. One night Don put the John Cleese classic *A Fish Called Wanda* on the video player and the four of us laughed until we wept. For the first time since I had been beaten, more than four months earlier, the tension, anger, sadness, and fear that I had buried inside began to dissipate with each peal of laughter.

Every morning after a lazy breakfast, I helped John do his stretching exercises, a three-year prescription meant to counteract the fusion of his vertebrae that had begun after his last operation in Munich. Then the four of us descended to the pool, for laps, naps, newspapers, and talk. Toward lunchtime we would wander barefoot along the sand to a simple shack of a restaurant on the beach, long gone now after a hurricane tore it off its foundations. We would eat stone crabs or hamburgers and drink a beer in the sunshine, easily talking and laughing together, just as we always had. We would down a piece or two of genuine Key lime pie, then stroll back to the Schanches' flat, unwinding a bit more day by day. Before our week was up, Don and Marybelle organized a joint birthday celebration, for John and I nearly share a birthday. One friend brought an armload of helium balloons attached to long, colorful, curling ribbons. She let them loose in the Schanches' big white living room, where they bounced around the ceiling in time to the ebb and flow of the air conditioner's fan. John still could not sit up very long, so after eating quickly he retired to the floor, where he lay on his stomach under the balloons. When the rest of us finished our dinner, we followed Don's suggestion and stretched out on the floor with John. It is possible to drink Champagne while lying on one's side, leaning on one's elbow, but it is not easy. We drank and laughed, always horizontal. We ate birthday cake and laughed, still horizontal.

By the time we got vertical again, I dared to let myself think that the worst of the nightmare might be over. It looked for all the world as if we would make our target date of mid-April to head back to work—and life as we'd known it. I knew we would both feel infinitely better once we could return to some semblance of normal life. We needed to have our days marked not by doctor's visits and lab tests but by headlines and deadlines, interviews and articles. We needed our nights marked not by nightmares and fear but by music and books; long, lazy walks; and time in each other's arms.

Our week in Florida finished, we flew to New York for what we thought would be a last round of family visits before heading back to Europe and John's new posting in Berlin. The *Times* had decided shortly after the shooting that John should trade his Warsaw posting, which involved heavy travel, for Berlin, which did not. But just as we dared to feel we were climbing out of our abyss, the light at the surface beginning to warm our faces, John fell terribly ill once more. The diagnosis was hepatitis B, caused by tainted blood transfused during one of his last operations in Munich. Neither of us had ever had hepatitis, but my mother's family doctor warned us that it would not be pleasant. Worse yet, there was no treatment other than luck and the passage of time.

Through that spring John became sicker and sicker, suffering all the typical symptoms of this disabling liver disease, which causes profound exhaustion and wreaks havoc on the body's digestive system and internal clock. His urine turned brown, his stool white. His skin itched until it bled. He suddenly lost his ability to sleep at night and would doze fitfully all day long, only to wake up, nervous and tetchy, as the sun went down.

Within days, John went cranky and quiet. I went cranky and loud. No hospital, no drugs, no treatment this time, just rest and a light, fat-free diet. But even though he followed all medical instructions, John's liver count kept climbing week after week until the doctor began broaching the possibility of a liver transplant if his condition did not begin improving soon.

It was my mother, who knew about these things, who pulled me aside one day when John was sleeping and suggested that John was not just sick but depressed as well. I argued against it, reminding her that the doctor had warned us that the symptoms of hepatitis B often mimic those of depression. I had conveniently put aside the doctor's other statement, that hepatitis B can kick-start depression. Uncharacteristically, my mother did not argue with me, but it was clear that she was deeply troubled.

When John fell ill, we had to cancel our usual summer plans to spend a month in our beloved lake house in Italy. We had been renting that house in Trevignano Romano every summer since we'd moved to Poland, and our time there was something that we and the children had come to count on. Part of the magic of the place was the presence of our close friends Ann and Joseph Natanson, who had discovered Trevignano when their two children were small and decided to build two nearly identical homes on a hillside plot they owned there: one for their family and one for guests. Ann, who is English, was Rome correspondent for Time-Life Books; Joseph, Polish, was a painter who had retired after years of working with Europe's top directors at Cinecittà, Italy's Hollywood. Both John and I were bitterly disappointed that John's hepatitis meant we wouldn't be able to see Ann and Joseph as planned, or lose ourselves in the simple, restorative rhythms of our summertime rituals in Trevignano.

Instead, we rented an old-fashioned cottage for a month at Fairfield Beach on Connecticut's southwestern shore, the beach of my childhood, where Peter and Anna would join us for the last two weeks of our stay. John and I packed our suitcases and

moved to the cottage in early June. A friend with a truck transported my childhood sailboat, an overgrown ironing board with
a green-and-white-striped nylon sail, to the cottage, too, so that
I could teach the children to sail. John lay in the cottage, dozing
by day, nervous and insomniac at night, talking little, eating less.
It was not until mid-June, just before the children arrived, that
his blood count finally tipped back in the direction of healing.
To this day I don't know if it was the doctor's talk about liver
transplants, the children's impending arrival, or simple coinci-
dence that turned the tide toward healing.

The photos we have of that time show John looking surprisingly well, considering what he had been through. Though his
hair had thinned and turned to straw, though he was undoubt-
edly bony, the weight loss made him look more like an aged
adolescent than a man not far from fifty. The scars, which ran
across his beltline, made wearing a belt uncomfortable, so he
had adopted suspenders to hold his trousers—baggy now—
in place. My favorite shot shows him clowning with Peter and
Anna around a picnic table, tufts of beach grass and the blue-gray
expanse of Long Island Sound in the background. Peter is hiding his eyes with a just-shucked ear of corn; Anna is holding a
half-shucked ear and happily sticking out her tongue. John is
looking like a hillbilly in oversized chinos held up too high by
a pair of blue suspenders. He mugs for me, behind the camera.
He's the one sporting the enormous handlebar mustache made
from a fresh tuft of corn silk.

9 ❦ Sütni Szalonna

Take one large hunk of Hungarian bacon, about the size of a large man's hand. Skewer it with a long-handled barbecue fork, then start a small wood fire out of doors, for *sütni szalonna* (pronounced SHUT-nee SULL-oh-nah) is a messy meal in the making and the eating. Once coals form, hold the skewered bacon over the flames until the meat starts to sear and melting fat begins to sputter on the coals. Cover thick slices of fresh Hungarian rye bread with a layer of chopped raw vegetables: sweet onions, garden tomatoes, and cucumbers. When heavenly meaty smells begin to emanate from the fire, press the blackening bacon and its dripping fat into a slice of prepared bread. The bread, which works as both plate and napkin, will sop up the runoff. Keep the bread slice parallel to the earth as you eat and avoid closing your eyes in bliss, lest the fat-drizzled vegetables slide to the ground. Repeat procedure. No matter how much you make, there will never be quite enough.

Hungarian farmworkers used to eat *sütni szalonna* in the fields during high summer, when the workday might start at four or five a.m. A few hours later, when the sun was well up and they were ravenous, they would eat a quick but nourishing breakfast in the fields, to avoid wasting time in trekking back home. Later it became a favorite picnic treat, which is how I first came to eat it, in the big backyard of our Hungarian next-door neighbors, whose sons, Johnny and Bobby, were my after-school playmates. Mrs. Vincze would prepare the bread and vegetables, and her husband would organize the fire, then skewer and cook the meat. The boys, their older sister, and I would stand by hungrily, salivating as the smoke from the sizzling bacon wafted skyward. No picnic food ever tasted so good to me as that Hungarian farmhand specialty, the cousin of Roman bruschetta or British bread and drippin'.

In 2007, when we spoke on a phone line that stretched from Paris to Rhode Island, Mrs. Vincze, well into her eighties, still sounded as bright and sharp as she had fifty years before. Trying to catch up on perhaps forty years of news, we both were thrilled to hear each other's voices. Our conversation seemed to jog her memories of my childhood in the two-family house that stood next to hers. "Your mother was so sick after you were born," Mrs. Vincze recalled without prompting, her accent still reflecting her Hungarian roots. "Your grandmother and your aunt used to come and take care of you because your mother couldn't."

Her simple explanation, uttered with empathy and kindness, hit me hard after I hung up. My mother had spoken of these illnesses to me only once; my aunt and grandmother never. Each of them, in her own way, was good with secrets. My mother's friends knew little if anything about it, and though a few may have known she had had some unidentified "problems" with childbirth, all of them seemed to have bought the picture she presented to the world: a plain-talking, loyal, and lively woman, both tiny and tough, who never appeared so happy as when she was ballroom dancing.

Even though I had known since my late twenties that my mother had suffered four bouts of postpartum psychosis, I had never really thought about what it had meant on a day-to-day basis for my infancy and childhood. I never dreamed her illness would have been so obvious to neighbors who lived across a stretch of two gardens separated by a chain-link fence. My mother's last bout of the baby blues ended a year after my brother was born, eighteen months before my parents bought a house of their own. All four of those collapses occurred in their sunlit rental flat, and it makes me wonder if at least some of the unfettered joy she experienced when we moved into a house of our own was not somehow connected to the idea that there she would find a refuge from the many fears that had plagued her.

Oh, how my mother loved having a home of her own! Whenever we would come into the house after a day or even a few hours away, she would turn the key in the lock, excitedly, yelling happily into the empty rooms, "Hello, house, we're home!" as if she were greeting a dear, long-lost member of the family.

My mother's fears were legion, though I did not know that when I was young, because she hid them so well behind various shields: gaiety, ferocity, silence, anger, and most of all, feigned normality. I always thought that one of her favorite lines— "We're so normal we're weird"—was meant as a statement of fact, not desire. She didn't tell me about her depressions until I was twenty-eight. She didn't tell me they had returned until another dozen years had passed. Her two revelations were both too little, too late.

Nine months after the shooting, we were still in America, waiting until John's doctors felt he had recuperated enough to return to work. He was not the only one impatient to get back. The truth was, I wanted John better yesterday. I wanted his liver count normal. I wanted his yellow eyes white. I wanted him bounding out of bed in the morning, as he always had. I wanted him giggling and teasing, gabbing incessantly. I wanted him dancing me around the kitchen, spouting Latin jokes. I wanted him wearing a belt, not those ridiculous suspenders. I wanted him looking into my eyes, not off into space. In short, I wanted John back, the man I married, so that we could return to the years-long honeymoon we had enjoyed before I was beaten, before he got shot. I was preternaturally impatient to get back to our real lives, not these fake lives we had been living, with him playing patient and me playing nurse.

John had no idea how impatient I was at the time, when my idea of a helpful spouse was still naiveté itself: patience, fortitude, endurance. Only now do I think that I was not acting like a spouse at all, but like a child, a child who watches her own mother suffering in a similar way but who feels powerless to help, afraid to do anything but watch and wait, lie low and hope.

We were fortunate that the editors at *The New York Times* could not have been more accommodating. They kept telling John to take his time and recuperate fully, though none of us truly understood how long that would take. But we were blessed that John's editors in New York had arranged for the Bonn bureau manager to find and set up a new office in a tree-lined neighborhood of West Berlin so that it would be ready when John arrived. It would have been beyond us both to even try.

Ever so slowly John's physical condition improved, while even more slowly he began withdrawing into himself. Although neither of us recognized he was slipping into depression until he was already there, his overall mood continued to slide imperceptibly downward and inward, worsening when I lost my job and the financial burdens fell more heavily to him, improving superficially and temporarily only when Peter and Anna were with us. Two summers after the shooting, we finally managed a visit to Trevignano with the children, with high hopes for what it might do for all of us.

But that longed-for vacation was cut short when John was called back to work early, to cover the revolution in Yugoslavia. There, exposed to the same kind of urban warfare he had seen in Romania, he began experiencing vivid flashbacks to the night he was shot. I begged him in nightly phone conversations to tell the foreign desk he had to leave, but he refused, saying he had to take the bad assignments with the good. Had I been listening to my heart and not to my head, I would have made the call to the desk myself and let them know what was going on. But I was afraid to interfere. I still feel that had I called then, had John been ordered out of harm's way before Yugoslav snipers started shooting in the streets of Zagreb as Romanian snipers had shot in the streets of Timişoara, we might have avoided years of woe. But I did not understand this at the time. I had yet to figure out what my role in John's recovery would have to be.

At precisely the same time John began experiencing flashbacks in Yugoslavia, my parents called me to say that my mother's clinical depression, which had been lying low for some thirty years, had returned unexpectedly. My mother—my own introduction to the woes that depression can bring to a family—tried everything her doctors prescribed. Electroshock therapy, which had unfailingly pulled her out of her earlier depressions, was out of fashion in the early 1990s, supplanted by new drugs that the big pharmaceutical concerns were churning out. My mother started medication immediately after seeking treatment, but after a few weeks her psychologist sent her to a psychiatrist, saying she was not responding and that she needed a doctor who himself could prescribe stronger drugs.

As the days and weeks of that sunny, warm autumn passed, it was soon clear that the new drugs were not braking her descent, but in fact hastening it. Like John, she too spiraled downward and inward until, in the middle of a mid-November night, she slipped out of the house and into the cold, black waters of Ash Creek, the saltwater tidal basin that lay at the foot of their street. By the time she was found, it was too late.

The shock of her death was worse than any of us could have imagined, a devastation of body and soul. "Heartsick," just a word or cliché before, took on an unutterable reality after. I lived, heartsick and unhinged, for months. When I think back to that time of violent grief, I think always of waves: waves of grief like body blows that started each morning before my eyes had opened; waves of pain that would convulse gut, heart, and head day after day, night after night. Were there waves slapping against the shore the night she slipped into the water? Or was the tide, as it so often did in that sheltered bay, rising silently, pulled by the moon, just as my mother was pulled into the water by her illness?

Months later, when I thought I had finally hit bottom, I realized with horror that my mother's death had taken on a virulent life of its own, infecting us all in our own ways. Her death helped push John back toward the depression he thought he had left safely behind the monastery walls three decades earlier. At the same time, however, her death would propel me to be on top of John's case, to remember always where depression could lead. In that way, I think, she helped save him, too.

Throughout that long, disturbing autumn of my mother's last bout with depression, I felt a growing ache to take her on my lap and in my arms as if she were a child, to hold her tight, to try communicating physically that she was not alone. When I think back on those unreal weeks, I see myself sitting on the floor of our Berlin bedroom, a phone receiver glued to my ear, night after night talking to my mother in Connecticut, night after night talking to John in whatever Eastern European hotel room he happened to be staying. It is tempting to think that my mother's full-blown depression made me miss the signals of John's incipient one. But I am certain I would have missed them in any case, just as my father had missed them at the beginning of my mother's descent. Perhaps we missed these initial warning signs because both John and my mother unwound quietly and at a crawl, because both were used to fighting depressive feelings on their own and hiding so well the ones they could not master.

But ignorance and the silence that surrounds mental illness played an enormous role, too. Neither my father nor I had ever seen the list—available these days on countless websites, in doctors' office pamphlet racks, in newspaper articles, in books—of textbook warning signs for depression. Neither of us knew such a list existed. And even though we had lived for decades with my mother's repeated bouts of depression, we both were still shockingly unaware of depression's potential power and fury. In fact, it may have been our basic familiarity with my mother's depressive collapses in the early 1950s, when she was young, that contributed to our inability to see that this one was different. In her first four brushes with the illness, my mother suffered mightily, but after electroshock she always pulled through. When she collapsed again, no longer young, we were worried about her health, not her life. And all of us accepted what the doctors told us at the time, that drugs were now the best, most enlightened treatment. If the medical community had begun to discover cases of drug-resistant depression, we certainly had never heard of it.

I could only make sense of a few basics. My utterly prudish mother had left the house in nothing but her nightgown. My mother, always cold and shivery, had gone out on a frigid, rainy night without a coat and boots and scarf and hat. My mother, who loathed cold water to the point of giving up swimming even in August, had willingly walked or jumped or dived into Ash Creek in the middle of November. My mother, who prayed on her knees nightly before getting into bed, who feared her God perhaps as much as she loved him, had broken the great taboo on taking her own life.

Intellectually I understood nothing about my mother's death at the time it happened, although intuitively I began to sense that her depression had been of a depth that only a fellow sufferer might have begun to imagine. Though the coroner's report of her death rightly and logically says suicide, my gut knows today that it was not my mother who took her life. It was the depression that took her life, the chemical imbalances in her brain that caused the depression that took her life. My mother, all five feet, one inch of her, fought heroically for most of her seventy-three years against those chemical imbalances. She battled silently and unceasingly, more than I ever really understood until long after her death.

It has taken me nearly twenty years to lose the denial, anger, anguish, terror, and confusion I felt after her death. It has taken me nearly twenty years to discover the depths of my admiration for the battle she waged. It has taken me nearly twenty years to be able to say, with pride and with love, that she fought like the tiny scrapper she was. *Ave!*

10 ❧ Fruit Salad

The Clam Box was Westport's premier fish restaurant for most of my childhood. An enormous hulk of a building, painted white with dark green trim, it sat high and dry on the old Post Road, a couple of miles from the beach. No clam shack catering to the beach crowd, it offered fresh lobsters, shrimp, scrod, turbot, sole, steamers in their own broth, tiny, fried little-neck clams, raw cherrystones, even finnan haddie for the odd sort who enjoyed his fish smoked.

Waitresses were generally middle-aged except for the summer help, twenty-one-year-olds drawn to the pricey restaurant by the potential tips. We all wore dowdy white dresses, dowdier white aprons, and sensible white nurses' shoes; long hair was pulled back off the face and coiled neatly into a bun or French twist. When Paul Newman and Joanne Woodward, who lived nearby, would slip in for an occasional meal, the white-haired Greek boss would immediately dispatch his eldest, dowdiest, and most circumspect waitress to their table. Even first-year servers like me knew that our job was not only not to stare, but to keep the occasional swooning fan at bay so that the Newmans could enjoy a good meal, undisturbed.

Except for the post-lunch lull, we were run off our feet on the job. But the tips were solid and I needed every nickel to pay for my first trip to Europe later that summer. Somehow my exhaustion would lift each night once I arrived home, sat down at the kitchen table with my parents, ate a dish of blueberries or a cut-up peach, and counted out my nightly take. I quickly found my rhythm, and the tips, the mainstay of my earnings, began piling up.

One night I got stuck with a client who had slipped past the radar of the chief hostess, the boss's tall, skinny daughter. A man of late middle age, alone, he was not the usual Clam Box patron, though in his crisp suit and rep tie he was dressed like one. Single guests, especially men who arrived half lit, were normally seated at the counter, apart from the main dining room, where they could be watched and kept from disturbing their neighbors. This man was trying his best to appear sober, but even I, who had seen only the occasional drunken boy at a prom, could see he was far gone.

Trying to focus his eyes, he rasped out his drink order in

a venomous whisper, a double Johnnie Walker Black on the rocks. He complained, in the softest of voices, about the size of the glass and the shape of the ice cubes when it arrived, then tasted it and quietly accused the house of pouring him a Johnnie Walker Red at the price of the Black. Glassy-eyed, he quietly demanded a second scotch while ordering his food, and complained bitterly in a low voice about every item I brought to his table, from the bread basket and salad, to dessert and coffee. Each time I approached, he would spew forth whispered vitriol. If I tried ignoring him, focusing on my four other tables, parties of four and six, he would threaten softly to "have my job." I never thought to alert the boss's daughter, and each time I had to deliver a new course or clear a plate from his table my stomach would knot.

By evening's end I was not expecting a tip, just another quiet onslaught when I brought him his change. But the large quantity of food he had eaten must have soaked up some of the scotch he had drunk, for suddenly he seemed to have sobered up. "Sorry," he mumbled, looking down at his hands. He left a wad of bills on the table before he walked out. Stuffing his tip uncounted into my apron pocket, I hurried to help with the usual cleanup once the last guests left.

I drove home seething and settled myself at the kitchen table with my mother and father, who always waited up for me. They liked to hear the stories of my day as I counted my tips, in those days much of it in small change. That night, I burst into tears as I told them about my drunk. My mother, always sensitive to frazzled nerves in anyone, suggested my father make me one of his Italian fruit salads while I figured my night's take, nearly $20 from my four normal tables. While my father was busy cutting fresh fruit into a soup bowl, I reached into my apron pocket and pulled out my last tip. My mother's eyes grew wide as I counted and kept counting: $26, far more than the cost of his meal, and a fortune for those days, when the minimum wage was $1.60 per hour. The windfall, however, had not been worth the *agida*, or aggravation, and my stomach started churning as my mind replayed the evening.

My mother tried to cheer me up, reminding me what I could do with a tip of that size, while my father whipped a few table-spoons of olive oil with lemon juice, salt, and lots of freshly ground black pepper to pour on the fruit. I can still hear my mother's voice that night, trying to draw out my frustration, coax my tears away. I can still hear my father beating that sauce with a fork before he placed his fruit salad in front of me and joined my mother and me at the table. They were a formidable team when their children were involved, Team Butturini, as my brother would describe them when he grew up, a team with a game plan and determination. When we were good, both of them were always there, rooting us on; when we were bad, only one of them would play the heavy. Each of them believed that no child should ever have two parents angry with them at once. That night my mother coaxed me to talk and urged me to eat; my father cut up the fruit; they both watched me chew, both listened to me unwind, until by the end of the bowl I was no longer sputtering with indignation and pique. Once I had worked through that mountain of fruit, my anger was spent. I stuffed my night's take into the cigar box where I hoarded my tips, kissed them good night, went upstairs, and slept without the slightest difficulty.

I still make that fruit salad even if the sectioning of the orange and the peeling and slicing of the rest of the fruit all take time. Somehow it seems like time well spent, for as long as you have a sharp knife, it is the sort of routine kitchen work that both calms the spirit and sets the appetite in motion. What I like best is hearing the rhythmic clickety-clack of my fork—an echo of my father's—beating against the little blue-and-white Italian ceramic bowl I always use to make the sauce. What I miss most is the sound of my mother's voice, trying to cheer me up. Even today I cannot eat that fruit salad without thinking of my mother sitting across from me at our kitchen table, and my father standing at the countertop, both of them listening to me rant about a drunken customer who left me a tip big enough to pay for my meals for nearly a week when I got to Paris.

My father came to Berlin to spend the rest of the winter with us, so that he wouldn't have to mourn alone in a small house that suddenly seemed too big. Near the end of his stay he was desperate for sunshine, and John, who had to travel for a week for work, urged the two of us to fly as far south as we could. We hopped a charter flight to southern Portugal, walked along cool but fiercely sunny beaches, ate in simple seaside restaurants. I can still taste the dry white port, served cold with a twist of lemon, that we drank as an aperitif that first night. It was the first time anything tasted good to me since my mother's death—the first time anything had a taste at all. Whatever freshly caught seafood we ate that night satisfied our hunger and soothed our soul. The cheerful noise of the restaurant helped, too, the easy laughter of the tables around us somehow helping to lighten our spirits. We ended that meal, and every other meal that week, with an enormous, juice-filled orange, freshly peeled and sliced into rounds at our table. Each time our waiter would cut the skin away—always in one continuous spiraling peel that would slowly bob up and down like an oversize Slinky—I would think back to our kitchen in Connecticut, where my father prepared his special Italian fruit salad for me that night twenty years earlier, where my mother was sitting across from me at our kitchen table, trying her best to make me forget my drunken client. By the end of that week, my father and I began to be able to talk again, about nothing and everything, the way we used to do at table before, before there was a "before" to consider.

It was in Portugal, four months after my mother's death, that

I first experienced the healing that can come from a beautiful place and its food, even if I wasn't yet fully aware of it. The strong winter sunshine; the cloudless, deep blue skies; the salt air; the laughing gulls; the feel of cold sand on tender winter feet; and the simple, good food served forth without pretense, prepared similarly to the way my father or mother or I might have cooked it at home: all of it helped put an end to the physical shock of my mother's death. The grieving, of course, had just begun, but it was no longer a grief fueled by adrenaline and physical panic. It may not sound like much, but it was my first real step out of shock.

John's own descent into clinical depression was so very gradual, creeping at such a lifelessly glacial pace, that I did not see it coming until long after it had arrived. When I think back now to that period, I see that John, normally sociable, jovial, and easygoing, an inveterate teller of hopelessly old-fashioned jokes, was increasingly withdrawing into himself. Normally never happier than when he was deep in work on a story, he seemed stressed, pained, and exhausted by his work, his usual effervescence and intellectual excitement gone. Normally thoughtful, caring, comforting, he seemed unable to look beyond his own nose. All pleasure had left him.

It remains galling to me even today that I was so blind to

PAULA BUTTURINI

what was occurring. My mother's death had so recently made
me see the degree to which I had misunderstood her, throughout my childhood and well into adulthood, had misunderstood
the role her clinical depressions had played in her complicated
nature and our complicated relationship. Now that I knew
the truth, how could I be so blind to the same disease in my
husband?

At the time it seemed to me as if it all happened in one weekend, a week before we were to move to yet another new posting,
this one in Chicago. We had already packed our things, flown
to the States, and signed a lease on an apartment. We were staying a few days at my father's house when John basically stopped
speaking and seemed to curl up inside himself; he had realized
too late that he was unable to put the Atlantic between him
and the children, unwilling to leave Europe after twenty-five
years. The move to Chicago was clearly that final drop of water
that makes a brimming glass spill over, an image doctors often
use to describe the onset of depression. The old, lively light in
John's eyes, which had been dimming since he began suffering
the effects of hepatitis B nearly two years earlier, simply went
out completely that weekend. Just as when he had had hepatitis, John's internal body clock was turned upside down, and
he began sleeping and dozing throughout the day, while lying
awake, usually in a panic, during the night. Sometimes he would
break into uncontrollable sobbing, sometimes he would simply
sleep or pretend to sleep or lie in bed, rigid, eyes closed, fists

126

clenched. He could not or would not talk, other than to make an occasional grunting response to a question. Once I alerted John's editor to the situation, the *Times* immediately gave John a reprieve, put our move on hold, and helped John begin treatment with a doctor in New York.

A friend gave me a reference for a doctor of my own, and the first time I walked into her office, I told her I needed to know whether I was about to slip into a depression myself. I gave her a quick recap of what had happened to us over the past couple of years; I told her that I was feeling extremely tense and nervous, to the point that I often felt light-headed, nearly dizzy, and that I had a sense at times of watching—warily and from outside myself—all that was going on in my life. In response to her questions, I told her I was still able to eat, still able to sleep and not particularly weepy. She listened intently, this older, gray-haired woman whom I instinctively took to, and what she told me kept me going for a very long time. She told me it was normal that I felt tense and nervous, given the number of extraordinarily painful events that had occurred in my life in recent years. She told me that what I needed, more than anything, was a change of luck. She and I talked several more times that spring and early summer, and her commonsense approach to our predicament never failed to calm my nerves.

And then, as July approached, John seized on the idea of flying to Italy for vacation to see if a return to Europe might help brake his descent into full-blown depression. His doctor agreed on two conditions: that John continue taking the medicines the doctor had prescribed, and that they talk regularly and often by telephone. Once John agreed, we quickly made plans to fly back to Rome, meet Peter and Anna, and head north to Trevignano Romano for our usual summer stay.

11 ❧ Soup

When I was little, I loathed the canned soups my mother occasionally served for Saturday lunch. Tomato soup had a sharp, cloying aftertaste that caught at the back of my throat. Campbell's Cream of Mushroom made me gag. I hated the soggy texture of the vegetables in Progresso's Minestrone enough to try to swallow them like pills, without chewing. I might grudgingly eat a small bowl of canned chicken soup with its mushy rice, but somehow, to me at least, all canned soups tasted more of the can or preservatives than they did of real food.

To this day, I don't know if I was spoiled by the honest taste of homemade soups or just plain spoiled. Perhaps I simply had an overdeveloped sense of taste. But I do know that until I turned seven or eight, if it wasn't my paternal grandmother's chicken soup, or my mother's copy of it—homemade, and often featuring one of my grandmother's worn-out hens—I simply could not get it down.

Decades later, even the thought of my grandmother's chicken soup still makes me close my eyes and take a deep breath of anticipation: clear, golden broth with all the fat skimmed off after the pot had spent the night chilling. Angelina's chicken soup smelled of onion, carrot, celery, celery leaves, garlic, handfuls of parsley, and a single bay leaf. It was served with tiny stars of store-bought pastina or, even better, with a few of her homemade fettuccine, chopped roughly into bite-size pieces and barely cooked.

At its best, my grandmother's chicken soup would come out of the fridge in a Jell-O-like state. I loved to watch it, thick and clear, all aquiver, as my mother or father ladled it out of the kettle into a smaller pot for heating. When the ladle dipped into our battered soup kettle, the soup sometimes made a sucking noise, which I loved to listen for when I was little. But what I liked best was the resounding, reassuring "plop" a ladleful of jelled chicken broth made when it fell into the smaller pot. I still don't understand how the gelatin in the bones of the chicken necks and backs leach out into the soup, but I knew even then that it was the one thing in the world I liked best to eat.

Later, I fell in love with the rest of the family repertoire of homemade soups: my grandmother's bean soup, started with salt pork, onions, carrots, and celery, minced together so finely that it turned into a paste; my mother's split-pea soup, made only after a holiday supper yielded a meaty ham bone; her turkey soup, dark, strong, and made only once a year, after the Thanksgiving carcass had been picked nearly clean; and finally her onion soup, made with a mountain of finely sliced onions that sweated and cooked over the lowest of flames, then simmered in quarts of her best broth. Each of those soups filled the entire house with its own aroma and whetted my appetite so sharply that often I had to beg a tiny bowl of it before we sat down to eat.

I still have the recipes for all those soups, and like all the cooking of my childhood, adolescence, and early adulthood, recipes—precise recipes—existed for just about everything any of us made. My mother cooked by the book. My father cooked by the book. And I, even in first grade, cooked by the book. I still have my yellowing children's cookbooks, in tatters now: *Mary Alden's Cookbook for Children*, which must have been put out by Quaker, as nearly every other recipe includes Quaker-brand oats, cornmeal, or puffed wheat; and *Betty Crocker's Cookbook for Boys and Girls*, a first edition from General Mills, whose recipes feature the brand's flours, not to mention its mixes for cakes, muffins, biscuits, and frostings. I cooked my way through both of those books by the time I was ten, and my mother made my children's meatloaf recipe for decades. We both learned early to avoid any recipe pretending to be Italian; neither the Quaker man nor Betty Crocker had a clue to Italian food.

The first supper I ever made for my mother and me—strategically planned so that the initial efforts of a seven-year-old

PAULA BUTTURINI

occurred on the one night a month my father had a dinner meeting—came from Betty Crocker. My mother, famous for her impatience, had the great good sense to leave me alone in the kitchen. She retired to the living room, where she promised to be available to field any questions. Alone then, I browned chopped onion, ground beef, and salt in a tablespoon of fat, sprinkled the mixture with flour, then cooked it briefly with milk. Served over mashed potatoes, "Saucy Hamburger Crumble" disappointed as much as it delighted. Nearly fifty years later, my shame over the look of the gloppy, gray goo that I had produced nearly overpowered my pride in having actually cooked an entire supper by myself. Despite its blandness, the meal didn't taste half as bad as it looked. Even a bad recipe has its uses: "Saucy Hamburger Crumble" was an unforgettable way to learn that food tastes better when it looks appealing.

When we landed at Rome's airport shortly after dawn, John was deeply and clinically depressed, heavily medicated, still half asleep from the long overnight flight. His eyes—not his own eyes, but a stranger's eyes that had mysteriously taken up residence in his head—sometimes glittered as they darted nervously from side to side. At other times, these stranger's eyes—at once terrified and terrifying—appeared dull, lifeless, and unseeing, as if they were turned so far inward that no light from the outer world could possibly find its way in.

132

Waiting for Peter and Anna's flight to arrive from Germany, John was trying his utmost to appear "normal" or at least as "normal" as possible under the circumstances. But his agitation was palpable. He ground his teeth. He did not speak. He worked his lips nervously, pursing and relaxing them uncontrollably. Even when the children appeared, his smile was, like his eyes, a stranger's, crooked and frozen. But the children hugged and kissed him willy-nilly, and we managed to find our rental car and pile our four small bags into its tiny trunk. We headed northeast, past the welcoming umbrella pines that still line the airport approach road, past the herds of fat sheep that used to graze on the parched fields, past the red-tiled roofs of old stone farmhouses that have since given way to high-tech factories and office buildings.

I do not remember if we sang on the way, as we always did (and still do), the songs and nursery rhymes of the children's babyhood: "Froggy Would A-Wooing Go," "Goosey, Goosey, Gander," "I Know an Old Woman Who Swallowed a Fly," an hour's worth of others. I do not remember if John spoke or slept, if the children were quiet or if they chattered.

All I remember is cresting the hill near the castle in Bracciano and seeing the sparkling lake spread out, round and crystalline blue, with our destination, the former fishing village of Trevignano Romano, on the far north side. I remember suddenly praying that the view; the house; the long talks and occasional dinners shared with our friends Ann and Joseph; the mornings of reading, drawing, and Ping-Pong; the afternoons of swimming and reading on the beach; our long, lazy meals on our wisteria-choked terrace; our strolls along the lakeside promenade; our long nights of solid sleep—that each of the moments we had for years enjoyed there would somehow help John's horrors cease. As I drove along the winding lake road, I couldn't wait to restart our habitual lakeside rhythms: our late breakfasts and very late lunches; our daily descent to the beach when the sun was well past its peak; a quick stop in the village to pick up a few bits of food for dinner on the terrace, where we would watch the fierce light mellow, then slowly fail. Only then would we make our one important decision of the day—whether the evening's entertainment meant a round of Monopoly or another descent to the lake for a gelato and walk on the promenade before we went to bed. The Natansons' simple guesthouse, gray with light blue shutters, had neither television nor phone, but around bedtime, if the wind was right, we could just make out the sound of a Verdi opera floating over the dark garden from Joseph's ancient wooden radio. Neither of us ever found a better lullaby.

As soon as we drove onto the long, winding dirt track that led to Ann and Joseph's pie-shaped property, the hilltop's two resident dogs started barking their greetings and escorting the car. The chestnut trees—real chestnuts, not horse chestnuts—that lined the track already seemed weighted down with what appeared to be a bumper crop. The brambles were thick and dusty, and I could see a profusion of blackberries, not yet ripe. The little peach tree, which produced ugly but succulent fruit, perfect for jam, was loaded with small green globes. We could not yet see what Anna always called Apricot Heaven, the tiny orchard of gnarled apricot trees that stood on a sloping terrace below a high rock wall that ran just in front of the house. But once we kissed Ann and Joseph hello, once we unpacked and went out to explore, we saw that the apricot trees were groaning with ripe fruit and we heard the yellow jackets buzzing madly, drunk on apricot nectar.

That was the July I entirely gave up cooking by the book. I mean that literally; my recipes and cookbooks—not to mention our furniture and clothes and virtually all of our earthly belongings— were in dozens of cardboard cartons, packed in Berlin in April and now sitting in a warehouse in Virginia, waiting for word to be moved to Chicago. As it happened, everything we owned stayed in that Virginia warehouse for two and a half years.

But when I say that I stopped cooking by the book, I mean it figuratively as well. Everything about our old life seemed to be in storage, somewhere far, far away. Our old life—a life of incessant work, deadlines, stories, interviews, and research; a busy, fulfilling life bubbling over with the children, family, friends, concerts, plays, movies, travel, reading, exploring—was suddenly on hold. John's downward slide did not happen in a vacuum. Everything we had or knew or loved seemed bent on sliding down that dark, steep slope after him. We were here in Italy trying to stop that slide.

We tried to explain to Peter and Anna, seventeen and eleven then, that their daddy was ill, suffering a depression that was a delayed reaction to the shooting, though we had neither the vocabulary nor the expertise at that time to explain it very well. But even the youngest child is far wiser than most adults could ever believe, and if they did not always fully understand our attempts to explain their father's illness, they could see it clearly for themselves.

Their daddy, who normally would sing to them, tell them his own father's jokes from the 1930s, read to or with them, play Ping-Pong, sketch with Anna or talk world history with Peter, their normal daddy, the world's fastest and most precise Monopoly banker, suddenly wasn't there. He did not sing. Did not tell jokes. Could not read. Was too dizzy to play Ping-Pong, even in the shade. Had no interest in sketching. Or talking world history. Our prizewinning Monopoly banker could no longer make change, nor count out banknotes. He could not remember what he or anybody else had just said. Daddy's body was there but somehow Daddy was not. This impostor daddy had all he could do to stay awake and occasionally focus his eyes upon them.

That said, John never stopped trying to be in good form for the three weeks the children were with us. But as our July vacation neared its end, and Peter and Anna prepared to fly back to Bonn and we were to fly back to New York, John dug in his heels and announced that he could not and would not go back to the States. He told me he feared he would spiral downward out of control if he went back. He asked me to call the *Times'* executive editor in New York, Joe Lelyveld, and tell him that he felt his only chance at getting better lay in Italy, where he had spent so much happy time, where he would not be so far from Peter and Anna, where he, for whatever reason, felt somewhat safe.

Ann and Joseph had new guests arriving in August who would be staying the rest of the summer in the guesthouse we always rented. But they invited John and me to stay on as long as we liked in the extra bedroom of their own house, whose two windows looked out on their vineyard. John seized on their offer, and when I called New York, Joe agreed we could finish out the summer in Italy, to see if the sunshine, swimming, friends, and food might have a positive effect.

At the end of July, the children and I headed back to the airport, where I put them on the plane to Germany. I drove back to Trevignano slowly, with dread, knowing that all the energy John had expended trying to act as normal as possible for Peter and Anna—which was not normal at all, of course—would leave him doubly exhausted once they left.

He barely spoke when I returned. He packed his carry-on bag with his three knitted shirts, an extra pair of Bermudas, a pair of trousers, a bathing suit, and underwear, and carried it across the garden to our new quarters. I packed my little carry-on bag with my few things, cleaned up the house, and followed him.

It was a Sunday, and as usual, Ann and Joseph were serving up one of their standard lunchtime feasts, lasagne from the local pasta shop in the village and Ann's famous Stretchy Chicken, a large hen generally stuffed with sausage meat, cubes of dry bread, sage and parsley from the garden, and various bits—onions, garlic, and celery—from her vegetable bin. (Its name came from the skill of the carver, their son, Stephen, whose slim knife could stretch the meat from any hen to fit the number of guests.) We sat down with the rest of the crowd. I ate the lasagne and moved on to the chicken and green beans, which were followed by a huge green salad. I ate homemade apple tart with a spoonful of gelato on the side, then drank a tiny cup of decaffeinated *caffè*. Normally a big eater, John only picked at his food. The drugs he was taking for the depression played havoc with his digestion; a thin slice of chicken breast with a few forkfuls of boiled white rice was all he could handle.

After the meal, hosts and guests alike took the usual Sunday siesta, resting on lounge chairs, sofas, or beds in the cool of the thick-walled house or the shade of the plant-filled terrace. A short nap was the only thing possible in that fierce, midday August heat. Even the dogs slept. Only the honeybees droned on, the sole creatures capable of moving. Everybody else listened to their bodies and dozed, drowsy from the food, wine, heat, and sun. Later, when the worst of the heat had dissipated, we all gradually awakened, with that charge of energy that comes from a serious afternoon snooze. John alone remained lethargic, from the depression as much as from the drugs he was taking to fight it. Lethargic or not, we drove down the steeply curved mountain road to the lake, joining the rest of the Sunday bathers returning to the beach for a late-afternoon swim.

My father called me every Sunday afternoon of that difficult summer, when he had been diagnosed with prostate cancer, when my brother's childhood kidney disease had suddenly flared up. Week after week I had no good news to report, but my father always seemed to be able to dig down into his experience with my mother's depressions to find something to tell me to help me keep going. If I complained that the man I was living with was not the man I had married—that the man who never stopped talking, revealing, joking, laughing since we had met had suddenly gone silent in my presence, that all our old ease and delight had turned into awkwardness and dismay—my father's basic response was simple: "You've got to remember, it's not John doing this, it's the sickness." It was a phrase I found myself repeating, like a mantra, but initially at least with little conviction and through gritted teeth. Still, it was those calls from my father, and my brother, too, that I looked forward to all week, and that—along with the Natansons' attention—kept me from despair.

I wish I could say that I knew back then that Trevignano was the perfect potion for both of us, that it kept me cheerful and upbeat in the face of John's worsening illness, that it reminded me of all the happy summers we had spent there in the past. But I can't. Thinking of all our happy summers there in the past just brought home how unhappy I felt in that present, nine months after my mother's death. What I wanted was my old life, when my mother was alive, when I brought home a monthly paycheck from a job I loved, when I lived with my real husband, not some impostor. While I knew that no amount of Trevignano sunshine, no amount of Ann's good soup or Joseph's excellent conversation could magically grant any of my desires, I could still think of no better place to try to heal.

Unconsciously, I was using our large stock of good memories from Trevignano to push away my fears about what would come next, what we would do if *The New York Times'* institutional patience ran out before John healed. I found that if I focused only on the present, if I banished all thoughts of our suddenly uncertain future, I could get through a day. Each day I knew I just needed to get through that day. Nothing more. At some point I seemed to break it down even further. I had to get through the morning. I had to get through the afternoon. I had to get through the evening, and I had to get through the night. Meals punctuated the first three tasks, sleep the last. Without consciously knowing it, I began marking the passage of a day by its meals. Suppers began to mean that John and I both had gotten through another day.

Italian suppers are traditionally light since the main meal is usually eaten at midday, and Sundays in Trevignano usually ended with a bowl of Ann's trademark vegetable soup, followed by an omelet or a slice of ham, green salad, and finally, fresh fruit. I marveled at Ann's soups and how she would dig deep into the recesses of her tiny refrigerator or pantry and pull out all the bits and pieces of vegetables that had eluded her during the weekend and would not survive till she returned the following

Friday night. Ann would start whirling around her tiny kitchen, a sunny corner of the house's main room, madly chopping anything she could find: an onion, a wilted leek or two, three tired carrots, a stalk or two of celery, some leftover zucchini, maybe a bowl of green beans, a slightly wizened bell pepper, a handful of Swiss chard or spinach—anything and everything, save beets, got cut up Sunday evening, thrown into the bottom of her ancient pressure cooker with a bit of olive oil and handfuls of herbs from the garden, and sautéed quickly until lightly browned. Then she would add salt and pepper and cover it with plenty of cold water, seal the pot, and let it cook until we were all back at the table, eager to eat again as the evening coolness descended.

Ann's suppertime soups were always light, tasty, and unique, since the contents of her refrigerator differed from week to week. We used to joke that, like our old housekeeper in Poland, Ann could have made delicious soup even if she had access only to grass, herbs, and a few cups of clear water. Ann's intuitive style of cooking—a harum-scarum whipping up of whatever ingredients she happened to have on hand into a delicious soup, pasta sauce, or chicken stuffing—was anti-recipe, the opposite of the rigid cookbook method I had grown up with. Since all my cookbooks were locked in a warehouse in Virginia, it was exactly the sort of unintended cooking lesson I needed. Like Ann, I started improvising in the kitchen, just as we found ourselves improvising in our life. We didn't know it yet, but we were writing a new script for our new life.

At this point during his illness, John could barely speak, but Ann and Joseph and their grown children, Stephen and Phoebe, had a gift for talking to him as if nothing were wrong. Their ordinary conversations pulled John along, kept him in the orbit of normality, even if he felt that he was spinning out of control. Somehow their talk—from art and films to political gossip and worries about aphids on the roses or worms among the tomatoes—kept John tied to the reality of the present, even if he was hard pressed to respond. Tears could be welling in his eyes or running down his cheeks, but Ann or Joseph or Phoebe or Stephen would just carry on talking to him as if those tears were not there. Their redoubled chatter, whatever John's mental state, was, perhaps paradoxically, a sign of their deepest care.

Joseph was especially gifted at drawing John out of the blackness that assailed him. A born raconteur, his intellectual barnstorming had been honed by his father, who required each of his four children to deliver at least one amusing story per meal. Though born into an old banking family in Poland, Joseph was studying art history at l'Ecole du Louvre in Paris when World War II broke out. He joined the Polish Army in exile and was among the Allied forces evacuated from Norway after the battle of Narvik in June 1940. Two of Joseph's three sisters were still alive, in Poland, but he had vowed not to return as long as the Communists were in power. Now that the Communists had been ousted, he was already toying with the idea of mounting a traveling exhibition of his paintings throughout the country.

Joseph, whose slender, six-foot-four frame was crowned by a mop of silver hair, loved to carry on long and, given John's silence, mostly one-sided conversations with John, sometimes in Polish, or Italian, or English, and often in all three. Joseph was working halfheartedly on a book of memoirs, and in the years before John became ill, he loved to pick John's brain about the new Poland while telling him about his own youth in Warsaw and Kraków. Joseph, eighty-three that summer, talked readily about his life in Scotland and England after the war, when he had written books cataloguing Gothic and early Christian ivories. After working in London on *The Red Shoes* in 1948, he moved to Rome to work on special painted effects in more than eighty films, from *Two Women* to *The Name of the Rose*, with directors such as Fellini, Zeffirelli, Pasolini, and his beloved De Sica. Joseph spoke endlessly and lovingly about his favorite novelists, such as the Brazilian Jorge Amado, and scornfully about abstract painters, whom he judged incapable of producing representational art. Only when coaxed would he discuss his own paintings and sketches: portraits, landscapes, still lifes and surreal dreamscapes.

During these endless weeks of illness, when summer slowly leached into fall, John remembers encouraging Joseph to push ahead on his memoirs, even though neither Ann nor the children spoke a word of Polish, in which he was writing them. To encourage Joseph, as well as to give himself a pastime during his illness, John began translating into English the neatly typewritten chapters Joseph already had completed. Joseph never asked him to take on this project, which was crucial, since it meant that the task was stress-free, done not under orders but for the sheer joy of exercising the brain.

John would spend an hour or so each day up in the bedroom loft that had been Stephen and Phoebe's room when they were little, sitting at a small table and speaking his translation into an old tape recorder Phoebe had found for him. The idea was not so much to give the family an idea of what Joseph was writing but to give John the opportunity to benefit from the power of good work. Those taped translations, quivery voice and all, helped John lose himself for short periods and lessened the force of his affliction. It was a labor that took him out of his illness and briefly placed him back among the healthy, rather than among the tormented.

Joseph eventually finished his memoirs, but endless delays by his Polish publisher prevented him from ever seeing them in print. The book came out in Poland shortly before he died in 2003, at the age of ninety-four, and a copy arrived in Rome just after his funeral. Phoebe later sent us our own copy of the book, telling us that Joseph basically wrote it for John, since John was his only real reader and the only one who encouraged him to finish it.

During the three months that John and I lived in Ann and Joseph's sunlit basement bedroom, Joseph's constant telling of stories, memories, tales, and adventures—related whether John answered or not—never let John completely slip away into the darkness of his thoughts. Normally Ann, Stephen, and Phoebe had to return to Rome to work, but Joseph, long retired, remained at Trevignano most of the time, painting, tending his vineyard, making the family wine, overseeing the olive harvest, doing endless chores from morning till night.

During our stay, Joseph spent less time than usual puttering in his vineyard or inspecting his few olive trees, his small apricot orchard, or his beehives, since he spent long periods of the day talking with John. The two men, both long and lanky, three decades apart in age, would sit like bookends on the shady terrace or inside the house's big common room. Joseph's voice produced a steady murmur, punctuated by an occasional hoot of laughter. That John was largely incapable of contributing much to the conversation did not seem to trouble Joseph, who was generally happy in front of an intelligent audience, no matter how small. They would break off reluctantly when chores finally called, though John began helping Joseph, as much as Joseph would let him, repairing the odd lamp or handing Joseph the tools needed to fix an errant grapevine. Like the translating of Joseph's memoirs, it was stress-free busywork that was an enormous help in getting John through the day without panic.

John and I quickly fell into a routine of meeting Joseph on the terrace that overlooked the lake to eat our meals together. We started around eight, with thick slices of crusty country bread, with butter and jams from the garden's fruit trees, perhaps a bit of cheese or yogurt with honey from the hives that stood below the house, and mugs of strong, milky tea. After working in the garden or doing other small chores, we met again for "elevenses," milky coffee and a couple of simple, store-bought butter cookies, so we could keep our hunger at bay till the main midday meal about one p.m. I happily took on the cooking: a simple pasta or risotto to start; then some sautéed veal or chicken and a vegetable from the garden; a green salad tossed with olive oil, lemon, and sugar—as Joseph liked it—then fruit, followed by the inevitable siesta.

After we awakened, I would drive John down to town, where we would walk along the lake in silence—he was unable to talk with me, although sometimes he managed to respond briefly to an occasional question. Sometimes we would take a short swim. As evening came on, we would drive back up to Ann and Joseph's property, and I would prepare a small meal, usually starting with one of the many *minestrine*, light water- or broth-based vegetable soups that I was beginning to throw together, as Ann did. John could barely get down a few mouthfuls.

The drugs he was taking—various combinations were tried and rejected, as one after the other provided no relief from the blackness he felt—played havoc with his digestion. The doctors never found a drug or combination of drugs that lightened John's depression. Eventually John's doctor in New York, with whom he was having twice-weekly therapy sessions by phone, began explaining to us the concept of drug-resistant depression, a surprisingly widespread variant that the big drug companies do not often address in their advertising. But the doctor felt it was wise to continue experimenting with various drugs in the hope that one would finally kick in and alleviate the worst of

John's symptoms. In the end, the only drugs that ever did what they were meant to do were old-fashioned antianxiety medicines, useful in moments of crisis. Like my mother, John had been helped by electroconvulsive therapy during his original depression thirty years earlier, but the treatment was no longer available in Italy, which in the interim had banned its use.

Although Joseph always turned in early, he loved to listen to opera while propped up in bed reading. When Joseph said good night, John and I would head downstairs to our bedroom, past the sage plant that was as big as an old Volkswagen Beetle, just off the main cellar workshop. The workshop was filled from floor to ceiling with tools, paints, art supplies, winemaking equipment, lawn mowers, easels, workbenches, ladders; endless boxes and jars of screws, nails, bolts, and washers; and a general hodgepodge of miscellaneous gear.

Every night as we descended those stairs to get ready for bed, I could feel myself seize up. During the daytime I, like John, could distract myself from our situation; there was nothing like weeding a garden or preparing a meal or reading a fat book in the shade of a tree to focus my mind on the here and now, to head off worries about some possibly frightening future. But whenever I wasn't distracted, I was finding it near impossible to be around John, for his collapse into suffering and silence unnerved me profoundly. I knew the man I had married was at least temporarily gone; I could not bear to think I might have lost him forever. I had just lost my mother forever to the same illness; it seemed damnably unfair that I was facing it again so soon, this time with my husband.

It never occurred to me at that point to think about leaving John because he had become ill; I had promised long before we took our official marriage vows that I would never let him drift off into aloneness as he had in Germany. That promise, more than anything, is what likely kept us together, along with the fiercely stubborn streak I had so grudgingly admired in my father's mother. Also at play was my own divorce. When my first husband told me he wanted out, my sense of self was shattered. I didn't want to change roles and walk out on John.

My parents' relationship must have affected my thinking, too, though it wasn't something I thought about consciously. Still, I could not imagine how helpless my mother would have been had my father left her when I was born and she first took ill. And even though I did not yet understand my father's halting steps toward getting over my mother's death, I could sense that he was on the right path when he began explaining how—despite the finale—his marriage to my mother had in the ultimate reckoning been a warm, happy, and productive union—Team Butturini, as my brother liked to say.

How lucky John and I were to have older long-married friends, such as the Schanches in Florida and Ann and Joseph in Italy! These were friends whose marriages had never been of the garden variety, friends who were bighearted enough, open enough, warm enough to take us in when we needed somewhere to stay, friends who fed us, feted us, unconsciously reminded us of the worth of battling together through whatever came along. How lucky we were that Ann could shout at Joseph on occasion when he wouldn't let her get a word in edgewise, how lucky we were to see him switch from petulance to delight at the words he finally heard her say. To be a comfort to one's spouse, to be comforted by one's spouse, to delight—and to growl—at one's beloved, to find joy in both the delighting and the growling: that is my idea of a sturdy, happy marriage. When it works, it is like a prayer: finding and being utterly oneself and communicating that true self to another.

How lucky we were to have had those months of heat and sun with Ann and Joseph, where daytime was a balm. Outside, in the ever-present strong sunshine, as I weeded a patch of garden, picked a few ripe tomatoes for lunch, or briefly lost myself in a book, I could have moments of near peace. Just as John, listening to Joseph during their frequent daytime meetings, could be brought out of the darkness within him, toward the real world of light.

Upstairs, in the light, with Ann and Joseph, I felt safe and supported, never abandoned. But as night came on, as we descended the steps to the cellar, all the terror I saw in John's eyes—or, better said, all the terror I saw in the eyes of that stranger masquerading as my husband—came flooding into my head.

In the daytime our bedroom felt absolutely cheerful, the walls covered with half a dozen of Joseph's early paintings, the sun pouring in through its two wide windows, which faced southwest, toward the vineyards, from which Joseph always made the family wine. I had grown up around the maze of my grandfather's grapevines and had never given them a second thought. But at night, Joseph's vines, far more gnarled than Joseph himself, even if less than half his age, turned sinister for me. Every time I closed my eyes in that room I would dream about those vines. In nightmare after nightmare I saw myself coming around a corner of the house and finding John's body, stiff and lifeless, hanging off some improbably tall branch, his limbs as twisted and gnarled as the grapevines themselves. Even in daylight, I was afraid of opening the cellar door and finding John's body, swaying slightly off a jerry-rigged scaffold. By nightfall I was terrified, even when we descended those stairs together.

I do not know why my mind was so focused on death by hanging. The lake, extraordinarily deep, would seem a more likely possibility for someone thinking about taking his life. Romans flock to the sea in summer, and largely avoid lakes, viewing them as sad, gloomy spots. Perhaps it was my mother's death by drowning that kept me from envisioning John's lifeless body floating facedown close to shore; I had already been down that road and could not even imagine going down it again. All I know is that when my fears for his life surfaced, it was always a hanging body my mind summoned forth. A friend once suggested that it might have been that John's depression, like my mother's, loomed like a noose around my own neck—and life. But I can't say for sure.

Neither of us slept well those weeks, no matter how much manual labor we accomplished during the day. We were eager to help Joseph with his chores, to pay him and Ann back at least partly for their kindness in letting us stay on with them. But I think we also were hoping that some of the heavy garden work, coupled with the walks by the lake and the afternoon swims, might translate into more tranquil nights, some restful sleep, an easing of the nightmares that haunted us both. As it happened, physical effort was a pointless exercise. No matter how much we tried to wear ourselves out during the day, our nights remained a terror, the heavy, leaden frame for an endless series of horrors dreamed, horrors dreaded.

Nightmares aside, John's memories of those months in Trevignano are remarkably positive, given his clinical depression, and certainly more positive than mine. He can remember the psychological terrors of those weeks and the myriad side effects of the drugs he was taking: the stomach pains, the digestive complaints, the skin eruptions, the frequent episodes when his upper lip would suddenly blow up like a balloon. But today his mind focuses elsewhere when he recalls those endless summer-to-fall days: on digging and raking in the gardens, on picking the grapes, on helping Joseph make wine, on listening to Joseph's reminiscences, on forcing his mind to translate Joseph's memoirs. As black as he felt, it was also paradise, he tells me. Joseph was his medicine, he says.

Our minds remember differently. When John recalls our

late-afternoon walks on the lakeside promenade, he remembers the glorious golden light of a day in early fall, the way it played and sparkled on the choppy waves that appeared like clockwork with the *ponentino*, the freshening little west wind that blows up dependably toward the end of the day.

My memories of those three months in Trevignano are more complicated. I have fond memories of Ann whirling about in her kitchen, talking about photography or lamenting the state of her tennis game, even as her hands flew and she threw together a fabulous meal. I loved seeing Joseph work at his easel, watching the oils he dabbed on the canvas turn so quickly into a vivid forest scene filled with four girls, hair flying and arms linked, as they danced in the golden light that filtered through the trees. I loved the relief I felt when I would hear John's voice upstairs in the loft, forcing himself to concentrate on Joseph's memoirs.

But it was also the time and place where I realized that John appeared to be nearly as sick as my mother had been, where I began to fear that he could end up as she had, a suicide. As summer began to turn to autumn, it was also the place where I began to worry what my role should be when it was time to take a new step forward, knowing that we couldn't simply hide out in Trevignano indefinitely. I felt powerless and trapped, and thought my only weapon was a frightened patience. But my anger, which I had managed to keep in check all these months, began to make itself felt, too. I just didn't know yet that anger, righteous anger, might have its own role to play.

12 ❧ Pizza

Most Friday evenings of my childhood, my mother and I performed the same ritual, driving across town to her parents' tiny apartment to pick up a week's worth of meat and eggs. The meat came from Gabriel's Meat Market, run by Cousin Paul's paternal grandparents; the eggs from the chicken and goat farm in nearby Easton, run by my mother's cousin Josephine and her husband, Bob, the only Connecticut Yankee in our extended family.

I loved going to that apartment for many reasons, in part because my grandfather Tony might be wearing his policeman's uniform, eating early so that he could go to work as a special cop at one of Bridgeport's many movie houses. He would always put down his fork to say "Hi, doll" and give me a bear hug. A strong but plump man with bulging biceps, he gave hugs that felt like pillows, different from the hugs I usually received from my father, who was affectionate but bony. I also loved visiting there because my mother's parents were easygoing and cheerful, and there was nothing they liked more than to shower treats upon their grandchildren. Every week we each got a quarter, to be put into our savings account, and later, when their weekly donation doubled, we got to keep the second quarter to spend as we liked.

My mother and I always left their apartment loaded down with goodies: the meat and eggs my mother had ordered the night before; a tin or two of Jennie's homemade spritz; the Swedish butter cookies that somehow had ended up in her repertoire of baked goods; a tin of her peanut butter cookies, still bearing the marks of the tines of her fork. Sometimes, in season, we walked out with a dozen of her fresh blueberry muffins. Other weeks it might have been an entire pan of brownies wrapped in foil, or half an apple pie, or her sour cream coffee cake—which I still make—topped and filled with walnuts, cinnamon, and sugar. In the summer, Jennie always threw in extra produce from their miniature garden, a couple of tomatoes or green peppers.

But the best thing about going to their place on a Friday night was the possibility that Jennie might have made a traditional pizza for supper. All sorts of pizza used to appear on their table, perhaps because my mother's family came from Naples, the cradle of Italian pizza. I could take or leave the actual pizza, a flat, round pie slathered in tomato and cheese, but I couldn't resist her way of using up her leftover pizza dough to make *pizza fritta*. The minute we walked through the door, she would slip cherry-sized knobs of dough into a kettle of bubbling oil, where they would sizzle, puff up, and turn golden. When she lifted them out of the fryer, she would douse them with granulated sugar, which didn't melt but clung in crystals to the dough balls' hot surface. The sweet crunch of sugar played against the slightly salty softness of hot, fried dough, and my mother and I could never get enough of them.

And every Easter Sunday, a totally different sort of pizza, one meant to break the long Lenten fast, appeared on our breakfast table. It had a double crust like a calzone, but it was flatter and wider, shaped like a foot-long strudel. My grandmother called it "pizza gain," an Anglicized version of *pizza china* (KEE-nah), which in itself is dialect for *pizza ripiena*, filled pizza. "Pizza gain" was stuffed with many of the foods one could not eat during the forty-day Lenten fast: *prosciutto crudo*, dried sausage slices, fresh runny cheese, and hard grating cheese all mixed together with endless fresh eggs from cousin Josephine's farm. We would cut into them on Easter morning, and on every subsequent morning until they were gone, a treat so rich that two slim slices would make a meal. I loved the Russell Stover's pecan-studded caramel egg that my grandmother arranged to have appear in my Easter basket every year, but I would have traded that egg away in a heartbeat for a whole "pizza gain" of my own.

Occasionally on a Friday night when my grandfather was

working, Jennie, my mother, and I would go out for pizza. Our favorite pizza parlor in my grandmother's North End neighborhood had a sign outside that said *APIZZA*, which my grandmother and mother always pronounced ah-BEETS. We would order a huge wheel of a pie with tomato sauce, sausage, and cheese, to be shared three ways. Waiting hungrily for it to arrive, my mother would announce that this time she would be patient and not blister the roof of her mouth on the bubbling cheese. The vow would evaporate with the arrival of the pie, and she would inevitably bite too soon, the hot cheese blistering her mouth once again. "How can I wait when it smells so good?" was my mother's perpetual refrain.

My father's family, on the other hand, wouldn't go near it. Neither of my father's parents ever ate a pizza, either in America or in northern Italy, where the very idea was as foreign as sushi or fried rattlesnake. My father, who ate everything, also drew the line at pizza. He had tried it as a teenager and become so ill that for decades he resisted even going to restaurants where pizza was served. Nearing eighty, he finally admitted that it probably had been the schooners of beer he had downed on that adolescent outing to New Haven rather than the pizza itself that made him so violently ill.

Through my childhood, though, pizza was a border that my parents' families would never cross. Pizza—the totem of our differences—defined us, separated us, brought some of us together, kept the sum of us apart.

The heat of a Roman summer generally builds unceasingly from early May until the mid-August feast of Ferragosto. By mid-August, virtually all things green—save the cypresses and umbrella pines that make the landscape Roman—have long ago turned a sere golden brown, and one begins to doubt the very existence of clouds, of rain, of cold. Just before the holiday, Rome becomes a veritable ghost town, as the city's inhabitants head for long beach vacations along the country's limitless coasts. Then, seemingly without warning, about August 15, the sun-bleached skies turn gray, storm clouds scud across the sky, and the rains, finally, blessedly, begin to fall. Temperatures drop a few degrees during these few days, the summer torpor wanes, siestas shorten, and thoughts turn to the coming grape harvest, the purchase of school supplies, and the cold season ahead.

The ancient Romans celebrated these annual rains as the Feriae Augusti, proclaimed by Caesar Augustus to mark the start of his very own month. Centuries later, the Catholic Church deftly chose the same date to celebrate the Virgin's assumption into heaven; in other Catholic countries the feast is known as the Assumption, but in Italy it remains Caesar's feast, Ferragosto. Despite its imperial origins, the timing of the holiday likely started long before the Romans, when the Etruscans, Sabines, and Umbrians were still wandering Rome's seven hills. Statues of Mary may well be paraded through Roman streets on August 15, but the ancient rhythms of the impending end of summer and the ripening of autumnal fruits—grapes, chestnuts, and persimmons—are really what is at play.

Even though it will be weeks yet before vacationing Romans return to the city—school generally reopens in mid-September—once the thunderclouds of Ferragosto arrive, one knows instinctively that summer's end is not far off. It was just after Ferragosto 1992 that John asked me to place another call to the *Times'* executive editor, Joe Lelyveld, to ask another favor. John had made a glimmer of progress in Trevignano, but he was still desperately ill. He passionately felt that he would only tumble into an endless abyss if he returned to the States at summer's end. Could Joe find a way to let us stay on in Italy, where John had spent happy times working before, so he could try to pull himself together there?

Joe got back to us quickly, agreeing to let us stay on in Italy as long as we moved to Rome, where psychiatric help could easily be found and John could restart serious treatment for his depression rather than continuing piecemeal care as he had at the lake by phone from his doctor in New York. John's job description for the immediate future, Joe said, would not involve journalism but psychiatry, and he instructed us to find a small, furnished apartment in the city. For the time being John was to work full time with medical help until his depression lifted. He was not to even try returning to work until he and his Roman doctor, still to be found, judged him ready. In the meantime, the *Times* would continue to pay John his full salary, a decision that freed us from financial panic. Rome was cheaper than Berlin, and once I started freelancing again, we knew we could pay the bills.

Joe's granting of our request both calmed and terrified John, and alleviated many of my short-term worries. John was utterly relieved to know we could remain in Italy, but he was—like many victims of depression—also panicked at the thought of even the slightest change to his daily life. He would literally lose his breath at the thought of having to leave the security of our quiet country life in Trevignano and exchange it for the noise and bustle of Rome and the eventual return to the pressures of work. But for me, it felt like the first time since John had taken ill that we were no longer floating aimlessly; we now had a concrete plan for the foreseeable future. That the plan involved returning to Rome, where we had met, fallen in love, and married, where the two of us had worked, where we spoke the language and knew the story, only added to my sense of relief. More important than anything was the idea that we would be coming back to a place where we both felt thoroughly at home, and safe.

At some point during September we began driving into Rome to look for an apartment not far from the *Times'* bureau so John, once he was feeling stronger, could walk to and fro, avoiding the chaos of the city's traffic. Finally, after repeated trips, we found a simple flat on the Via Giulia, a block from the Tiber and a five-minute walk from the office.

On one of our searches, we stopped at the American consulate, which friends told us kept a running list of English-speaking doctors in the city, including psychologists and psychiatrists. We took the list back to Trevignano and studied it, looking for names that indicated an Anglo-Saxon medical background. High up on the list, since his surname began with a B, was the psychiatrist we eventually called first. We had an exploratory chat with him by telephone; his British accent reassured John that his treatment could take place in English. The doctor listened carefully, asked a few measured questions, and agreed to take John on once we moved to Rome.

Meanwhile, John and I got to stay in Trevignano a bit longer, until the Rome flat could become ours. I have vivid memories of those last couple of weeks in the country. In addition to our usual routine of sharing meals and taking afternoon naps, followed by long, lazy swims, we tried to help Joseph with any chores around the property that needed more than two hands. The physical work in itself offered a kind of recuperation. I remember hauling out of the cellar and into the sunshine the enormous plastic and wooden barrels Joseph used for crushing his grapes and fermenting his wine. We hosed spiderwebs and a year's worth of accumulated dust out of the plastic barrels, and the cleansing felt therapeutic. Then we repeatedly filled and emptied the wooden one with water so that the staves would swell and lock in the liquid that eventually would go inside. The last weekend of our stay, we helped with the amiable chaos of the family's annual grape harvest. Between the physical release and camaraderie, we were able to put our worries aside momentarily and let go in actual enjoyment.

Dressed in our worst clothes, John and I helped Joseph, Ann, Stephen, and Phoebe, and a couple of other family friends harvest the rows of purple grape that filled the gently sloping field to the west of the Natanson house. After sorting, we took turns climbing into one of the barrels and stomping the grapes; then we helped pour the sticky liquid into Joseph's plastic barrels, where it would ferment in the cellar, opposite our bedroom.

I took off my sandals that day, and after the first few moments of uneasiness—I had to banish the sensation, born no doubt from Halloween parties as a child, that my feet were somehow trampling eyeballs—I stomped away with the rest of the crowd, my toes and soles feeling the skins of the dark purple grapes sliding off the fruit till they hit the solid bottom of the barrel. It was a sticky, fruity, juicy, buggy afternoon when we stomped, wine therapy at its best, not from the drinking but from the making, in a crowd of friends eager to enjoy the day. Neither John nor I, both exhausted and exhilarated, wanted that long day to end. That wine-making weekend marked the end of our three-month stay. It was time for us to go back to the city, back to making another stab at real life.

Late the next morning, when we arrived, Rome was its usual mayhem and chaos compared to the birdsong and hush of our

Trevignano days. But once we carried our suitcases up the stairs to our new front door, our tiny apartment seemed cold, all echoes and silences, compared to the warm bustle and hubbub of the Natansons' lake house. We had each brought a single carry-on suitcase when we left New York in early July for what was to have been a monthlong vacation. Once we unpacked those two little bags, hung our few items of clothing on hangers, and tucked the rest into a chest of drawers, we had effectively moved in. We found ourselves looking at each other as if to say, "What now?"

I ran into each room, throwing open all seven of our windows. If we couldn't have the birdsong and hush from the lake house garden, if we couldn't have the warm bustle and hubbub of the Natansons' house in Trevignano, we would simply have to make do with the commotion and uproar of Rome. We were going to get honking cars, screeching buses, whining motorbikes, and the elevated decibel level of normal Roman conversations, whether we were ready for them or not.

It was not yet noon, so I knew I still had plenty of time to do some food shopping at the Campo dei Fiori, which was only a five-minute walk away. I knew that the waist-high wicker baskets and wooden shelves lining the Campo's bread shop would already be full: crusty round *pagnotte*, long *filoni*, flat *ciabatte*, slim *francesi*, and puffy *rosette*, the standard lunch rolls that look like full-blown cabbage roses and come with a giant air pocket inside, to stuff with salami or cheese or a slice of grilled eggplant.

The Campo's bakery is usually seething with customers, the most fanatic of whom may push their way in and out of the tiny shop twice a day to ensure a meal with just-baked bread. If I arrived at the right moment, one of the middle-aged countermen, in his white lab coat, might be en route from the oven room carrying the latest batch of *pizza bianca*, which the younger bakers, their shorts, T-shirts, hair, hands, and feet totally veiled in a floury mist, had just pulled from the blazing heat of the *forno*.

Roman bread, by and large still honest, contains no preservatives and remains truly fresh for only a few hours. *Pizza bianca*, the simplest of Roman breads, is the most fleeting of them all, with a shelf life counted in minutes. Worked into a yard-long, foot-wide sheet, it is dribbled with olive oil, a shaking of salt and a sprinkling of rosemary. Then it is baked, briefly, until golden. At its best, just out of the oven, it is thin but not too thin, with a crusty top and bottom, and a soft, almost chewy center that is neither greasy nor pretzel-dry. It is then that it possesses a natural lightness and rustic sweetness that tastes better than nearly anything in the world. But when it is carelessly made or has sat too long, it can turn tough, heavy, doughy, or even sour, as if angry at being ignored.

Pulled from the oven on a long-handled wooden paddle, it is hacked into rectangles while still warm and sized according to the customer's hunger. The huge baker's knife whacks off first a single piece, and then that piece in two. In one motion the counterman claps the oiled sides together and wraps waxed paper around the bottom of the bundle, to keep fingers from getting greasy and to permit immediate eating, even before money changes hands. The best Roman bakeries turn it out in enormous quantities all day long, to give shoppers something to nibble on as they do their daily marketing, to get students to and from school without feeling faint. The smallest Italian banknote in the early 1990s, a thousand-lire bill, then worth about seventy U.S. cents, used to buy a fair-sized slice, easily enough to tide one over till the next meal.

Like Roman students, I too had developed a *wool-eee* for *pizza bianca* before we moved to Warsaw. Long before I had even met John, I would leave the bakery with a day's worth of bread in my left hand and a slice of warm *pizza bianca* in my right, to eat on my way home. I used to wonder what it was that made a plain piece of baked bread dough taste so good. It wasn't just its flavor or texture, nor its golden color or slightly salty tang. I liked the ritual that came with it: the comforting warmth of the bakery in the quiet, slow-motion atmosphere before the crowds arrived; the countermen chatting softly and companionably among themselves; the murmured greetings when a regular customer arrived; the clean, sacramental smell of baking wheat; the golden color of the finished loaves heaped on golden pinewood shelves; the whacking sound of bread knife on breadboard. All combined, like a father's hand around a child's, to promise safety.

But *pizza bianca* was glorious, too, because it met some half-forgotten childhood standard of goodness. To eat a food reminiscent of some childhood treat, to eat a food that nudges strong childhood memories, is to return to the country, town, neighborhood, and family—to the very dinner table where we first encountered the edible world. "What is patriotism but the love of the good things we ate in our childhood?" the Chinese writer Lin Yutang asked last century. What else, indeed?

I bought two pieces, enough for a hasty lunch. I bought four very ripe figs too, and four slices of *prosciutto crudo*. I could slice the warm figs and serve them with the ham, accompanied by the *pizza bianca*. We wouldn't need another thing till supper. When I brought home the fixings for that first lunch in our new apartment, I had to spread it out on the bags in which I had carried it home, for the flat, though furnished, had nothing in the kitchen but stove, sink, and refrigerator. We went out to eat that night and the next, until we borrowed a car and drove to a discount shop on the edge of the city. We bought six of the most basic white restaurant plates and pasta bowls we could find and a half-dozen place settings of stainless steel cutlery. We bought one small and one large frying pan, a small saucepan, a spaghetti pot, a colander, a vegetable peeler, a cheese grater, a corkscrew, a can opener, and a good sharp kitchen knife that I still use to this day.

Via Giulia, the street where our flat was situated, was laid out during the Renaissance as an artery for pilgrims to the Vatican. Running just a block from the tree-lined Tiber, it is full of historic palazzi and overpriced antiques shops; before the marriage

that made her the Princess Casamassima, Henry James's celebrated heroine Christina Light lived in a palace just across the
road from our tiny flat. But despite our apartment's fine beamed
ceilings and the high sheen on the few bits of antique furniture
that graced our small rooms, I felt as if we were camping out.

Maybe that is why I threw myself back into the marketing
and cooking I had so loved about Rome when we had first lived
there. I prepared three meals a day that year in our narrow little
kitchen, after buying whatever looked good in the market each
morning. And like a potter centering clay on a spinning potter's
wheel, the mere act of cooking centered me, kept me close, available, ready to help, kept us fed, kept me sufficiently focused on
present tasks so that I wouldn't panic about the future, kept me
going through the slow passing of a string of bad days, weeks,
and months. Our friend Lou presented me with a doorstop of
a cookbook that year, *Il Talismano della Felicità*—The Talisman
of Happiness—one of Italy's food bibles. I never actually used
it that year, but I liked its heft and solidity, sitting alone on my
kitchen shelf. More than anything, I liked its name.

At the time of our move, I remained obtusely oblivious to
the depth of John's illness, still naively hoping that his depression would magically disappear as suddenly as it had seemed to
arrive, that once back in Rome, he would simply wake up one
morning like his old self, eager to bound out of bed and race off
to the office. Instead, despite intensive meetings with his new
psychiatrist, three times a week, despite the total support he was

receiving from his editors and colleagues at the *Times*, the move into the city only magnified the terrors and the darkness John was feeling.

Living an hour's drive north of Rome, on a crystalline lake surrounded by hillside pastures, had helped John block out the idea of work. Moving to Rome and living a five-minute walk away from the office meant the idea of work and duty, obligations and responsibilities, could not so easily be held at bay. Living with Joseph—a friend, not family—had also kept John on good behavior. Joseph's presence (like the children's presence) obliged John to put on the best face possible, no matter how bad he truly felt. Without that obligation, without a nonfamily audience, it seemed harder for John to put on the show of trying to soldier on. Didn't I deserve the same sort of "good behavior"? Of course. But I didn't realize it yet, or know how to demand it of him. That would come.

13 ❧ At Table

When I was little, my father, mother, brother and I ate virtually all our meals around a Shaker-style maple table, solid despite its spindly legs. If I do the math, I figure I ate nearly 15,000 meals at that kitchen table. It was just big enough to seat the four of us comfortably, and I never remember sitting at it alone. Even as I got older and often returned home late after swim team or softball practice or work, I never came home to an empty kitchen, which was where we always seemed to congregate. Even if my parents and brother had already finished their meal, they would return to the table to sit and talk with me as I ate the supper my mother had kept warm for me in the oven.

Grazing had not been invented back then, or if it had, it was a concept that had never made it past our door. We ate breakfasts together, the four of us seated around the kitchen table at seven-thirty a.m. Except for school days, when my brother and I brought sandwiches, fruit, and a cookie to school in brown paper bags, we ate lunch together as well, seated around the kitchen table shortly after noon.

My father's office was five minutes away, and he and my mother ate lunch together Monday through Friday, a togetherness my mother did not always find comforting. She regularly complained that by the time she had gotten the breakfast dishes washed, the beds made, and the house straightened, it was always just moments before noon, when my father would reappear, to eat his lunch with her and read through the mail and his *Wall Street Journal* until he had to return to work.

A few hours later, we were all back at the same table, unfailingly eating supper together: meat, vegetable, and starch on a dinner plate, followed by a green salad with oil and vinegar in little wooden bowls, and fruit, sometime topped with vanilla ice cream, for dessert.

My father's family had eaten practically every meal of their lives together as well, the four of them tucked into a corner of the simple kitchen my grandfather had fitted out with a bright blue gas stove whose rounded shape resembled that of a plump nineteenth-century woodstove. Their kitchen table was my grandmother's work space as well, since their turn-of-the-century kitchen had no counters or cabinets, only a narrow, sun-filled pantry full of handmade shelves. Angelina, my father's mother, would cover her kitchen table with an enormous wooden cutting board my grandfather had made, and I can still see and hear her beating a couple of eggs, warm from the henhouse, into a small hill of flour, making the tagliatelle, *maltagliati*, and *pappardelle* they loved to eat.

My mother's family was no different, always together around their kitchen table at mealtimes, though rarely the four of them alone. Nearly always some cousin, aunt, uncle, friend, or neighbor who happened to drop by when food might be in the process of being served sat with them as well, especially during the Depression. My mother's mother did not seem to worry if she had enough to go around. When the guests outnumbered the available food, my grandmother would simply fill everyone up with pancakes. My mother, who always loved to dance, would regularly tap-dance for the crowd after dessert was served, but when I was older she confessed that while she loved dancing, she had always hated the constant stream of uninvited guests that her own mother had loved. In her sixties, my mother was happy to make vats of soup and deliver them to the elderly couple ailing next door, but she never invited them to eat at her table. Still, her generosity seems to have rebounded on my father, now the oldest man on the block. His younger neighbors take care of him the way my mother took care of that earlier generation, mowing his lawn, shoveling his walk, bringing him meals.

Sitting around the family table, sharing meal after meal, was one of the few habits both my parents' families shared. Apples and oranges they were from the beginning. Apples and oranges they stayed as long as they lived.

My father's parents—blue-eyed, fair-skinned childhood blonds —had emigrated from northern Italy, near Verona, in the early 1900s. But neither hungered for a new life in *l'America*. Both sailed looking back toward shore. Leone Butturini and his bride, Angelina, had a sweeter dream than democracy or riches or freedom: they ached for land, potential fields of their own one day in the peach-growing village of Pescantina, where Leone was born. Though the money they so carefully saved and sent home was inadvertently lost through currency fluctuations after World War I, though they resided on and owned two city lots of Connecticut soil for the rest of their long lives, though he eventually even became an American citizen, they always stayed utterly Italian.

My mother's parents—brown-eyed, olive-skinned, with thick, dark hair and a few rogue genes that produced the occasional blue-eyed cousin—rarely looked backward. Indeed, Jennie Comparato had no Italy to look back to at all, being the first of her eleven siblings and half siblings to be born not in Naples but on Mulberry Street in New York. Her husband, Antonio, from the dirt-poor Neapolitan hinterland, went through immigration at Ellis Island in 1906 with his parents, sister, and older brother, Pietro. Antonio came out Tony. Pietro came out Pete. But Pete and his parents and sister came out with one last name, Tony with another. Both brothers spent the rest of their ninety-odd years arguing placidly, but pointedly, over who left immigration with the right family name. Neither ever established which was correct. Neither, in the end, truly cared. Considering themselves Americans, what did a final vowel really matter?

Two sets of grandparents, two separate worlds, my mother's parents embracing America, my father's parents ignoring it. My mother's mother smelled of Fabergé; my father's mother of Cocilana cough drops. My mother's mother wore snazzy high heels, sheer stockings, and fashionable dresses; my father's mother favored clunky lace-up shoes, thick cotton stockings, old-lady dresses before she was old.

My father's parents drank the wine my grandfather Leone made in the cellar from his own fat blue Concords, filled in with cases of California grapes. Leone's grapes grew on homemade iron-and-wire trellises that outlined their massive vegetable garden and formed a shady arbor over the heavy wooden table and benches he had built to eat their summer meals al fresco. My mother's parents, perhaps convinced that wine would brand them forever as hopeless greenhorns, drank, when they drank at all, "Blood Marys," as Tony always called them. We always ate and drank with my mother's family or with my father's family, never both sides of the family at once. They were just too different to spend time together.

For months after we moved into Rome, John would hide himself in our bedroom and sob or cry at some point or points nearly every day. I felt the little ground we had gained in Trevignano had been lost. A ringing phone—an emblem of the outside world, his old job and life—was the most likely event to provoke the floods of sobs and tears. Some days John's sobs and tears were howls, which rang and echoed through the flat. Some days his sobs and tears were silent, accompanied by a heaving chest, clenched fists, and occasionally by the hollow, horrifying sound of his banging his head against the iron bedstead or the bedroom wall. Some days the sobs and tears were muffled, when the sudden ring of our phone or doorbell caused such terror that he would burrow under the bedspread, pillows, blankets, and sheets, trembling uncontrollably until he felt the terror had passed.

Worse than the sobs and tears, though, was John's silence. From the time I met him until the time of the shooting, he had never once stopped talking. It was the quality and the quantity of his talk that so drew me to him in the first place, and to lose that part of him was to lose a lot. Now he might grunt an answer if I pressed him, he might nod, but he did not converse. Had he been a quiet sort before his illness, it might not have been so difficult. But John had always loved to chat and talk, kibitz, and joke. To me it seemed as if John's normal effervescent self had been surgically excised, leaving only the sullen, somber shell of a stranger I could no longer even recognize.

It made me sullen and somber, too, and frightened. I never really wondered at that time whether everybody whose spouse struggled with depression felt the same way I did. I never even thought to pose the question to my father, who had been through five bouts of my mother's recurring depression, who called me unfailingly every Sunday to talk for an hour. But even if I never posed the question directly, I know now that my father was trying to respond to my worries whenever I complained to him how difficult it was to live with someone who was, for all intents and purposes, no longer mentally there, and who no longer reacted as if I were there, either. "Just remember, Paula," he would repeat endlessly, in a voice filled with concern for the two of us, "it's not John, it's the sickness."

As days turned into weeks and weeks into months, I felt increasingly helpless with each new spasm of terror John suffered. He was usually in bed, trying to nap, when one of these episodes started. I would hear him from the living room or kitchen, doing his best not to make much noise as he keened into the bed linens. I would listen a bit at first, hoping the terror might just pass this time, but when it did not pass—and it never passed—I would go to him and try to calm him, with soft words or none at all. Often I simply encircled him with both my arms, an embrace meant to say he was not alone, that I would not let him go, that I would not let him be flung off into nothingness. But those embraces, I see only now, were meant as much for me as for him. If I held on tight enough, I hoped that he—and I—would hang on, too, and not be flung off this revolving globe the way my mother had been. If he hung on, maybe I could, too. The three meals I prepared for us and that we ate together each day were simply another kind of embrace, a way to remind him that he was not alone, that I was not abandoning him.

Nothing I ever said or did during these moments of panic and terror seemed to have any effect, positive or negative, on John. After a certain amount of time had passed, the terrors seemed to die away of themselves. John would slowly turn slightly less frantic, then perhaps catch his breath. Once he caught his breath, the panic might begin to recede; once the panic began to recede, then slowly his breathing might calm; once his breathing would calm, he might even fall asleep, or feign it, his eyes shut, but his body still rigid, as if waiting for the next onslaught.

The rigidity of his body during the height of these terrors in turn terrified me. I felt as if I were watching a horror movie, as if an alien being had slipped into my husband's soul and sucked his spirit dry, and left his body filled with wood, stone, metal, or concrete instead of blood and guts, the pulse of life. During these months, whenever John moved, he walked with the stiff, rocking gait of a B-movie horror monster. He lumbered and lurched when he moved, his knees locked or nearly locked, and he rocked first to the right, then to the left, as he swung his legs first outward, then forward with each step he took.

Because everything was still in storage, we had few belongings when we moved back to Rome from Trevignano, just three changes of summer clothes and the half-dozen bright yellow bath towels and the few bits of kitchenware we had bought when we moved in. Yet I found I rarely missed any of our stored belongings.

Our lack of possessions did not in any way mean that our daily life was simple, but rather that we had simplified our daily life. A much simplified life was all either of us could possibly handle, as we tried to make the psychological move from the vacationland security of Trevignano to the workaday chaos of Rome.

I never consciously chose to put aside my terror of what might be coming. I never consciously chose to stop looking ahead, as I always had, far into the future. But at some point, within weeks of moving back to *bella Roma*, I found that I was more comfortable when I looked only as far as three meals ahead of myself. Before I even knew what was happening, it seemed I had found my comfort wandering through the food stalls that lined the Campo dei Fiori.

Cooking was my way of trying to make us both feel at home again, to make us feel as safe and nourished as we did as children, when we ate all our meals surrounded by utter familiarity and routine. During that year on the Via Giulia, I went to the Campo six days a week, to multiply the good I took away from each visit. I bought enough food to last for a day, two at most. Everything we ate seemed to have been picked just the night before, just for us. During that year, I cooked every comfort food from my child-hood and John's: pastina in chicken broth for me, simple risotto or chicken baked with garlic, rosemary, and potato wedges for John. I bought every seasonal fruit and vegetable I could find; I catered to every *wool-eee* that made itself known.

Talking to the vendors at the Campo, I learned to make Roman comfort food, too: oversized tomatoes stuffed with rice and herbs, and baked with potatoes; *straccetti*, or "little rags," of tasty beef, barely cooked in hot olive oil with garlic slivers and fresh rosemary, then topped with fresh, peppery *rughetta*; baby artichokes braised in olive oil, water, and handfuls of parsley and wild fresh mint, the artichokes so small and well trimmed that we could eat them whole, along with the long, narrow stem. Even today, just the thought of those old Roman dishes makes me long for them and the strength they gave me to face another day. It was during that year on the Via Giulia that food solidified as an emblem for us, of good times remembered from childhood, of healing in that stretch of trouble, of promise that we would once again have a future to enjoy, if only we could hang on till the fever of depression passed.

Never mind that most days started badly, with a nightmare that would jerk me out of sleep so suddenly that it seemed as if a rifle had fired, a bomb had exploded, a siren had screamed in my brain. Never mind that my eyes would fly open in the darkness and I would awaken to find myself already sitting up, my hands in fists, my breath coming fast, one leg half out of the covers, ready for fight or flight, I never knew which. John would stir in his sleep at the commotion and I would lie back down, trying not to fidget while the dreams that had awakened me continued to run, fainter and fainter, in my head. For an hour I might lie there pretending to rest, but the effort would wake me so thoroughly that in the end there was nothing to do but get up and escape. I would dress, throw open the oversize bolts on our heavy front door, and walk the five minutes to the Campo.

Day after day, listening to the gulls and bells—for Rome, in the quiet of early morning, retains the medieval cacophony of a city of wheeling seagulls and pealing church bells—I would make my morning walk. Day after day, I found, my breathing would slow and my heart would stop racing shortly after I walked into that enormous cobblestoned rectangle of open space. It might have been the uncharacteristic hush of early morning that soothed me. It might have been the comparative calm of the merchants, who at that hour would be companionably stacking endless wooden or cardboard flats of fruits, greens, vegetables, and roots in relative silence, adjusting their dirty white tarps or huge *ombrelloni* to keep the sun or occasional rain at bay. All I am sure of is that by the time I arrived at the Campo, I felt better than when I had slipped out of the flat, leaving John to toss, moan, and shout in the last hour or so of his ever-restless sleep.

The sun would be up, throwing a soft half-light over the cobblestoned piazza. Some of the vendors would still be swallowing their morning shot of *caffè* as they unloaded the last of their produce. The oldest, the thick-fingered grandmothers in dark dresses whose children and grandchildren had long since taken over the running of the stand, would already be surrounded by cases of tangled, muddy greens: *rughetta, cicoria, spinaci, broccoletti, scarola*. These they would strip, trim, wash, pick over, and otherwise prepare for the pot until it was time to close for the day.

I liked the Campo best then, when the light in the square was soft and pink, when everyone in it seemed unnaturally subdued,

the vendors still fighting sleep rather than the demands of customers or the sun's fierce heat. Even at that hour, the smell of
wood smoke and just-baked bread would be seeping out of the
doors of the bakery at the northwest corner of the square. I
liked to stroll among the vendors first, not buying immediately
but searching out what looked best to bring home for that day.

A half-dozen fresh eggs, a bit of straw clinging to their shells.
We could eat a soft-boiled egg for breakfast, followed by thick
slices of crusty bread from the bakery. Jam, for John, we had, but
maybe some more butter from the dairy shop, along with a slice of
Gorgonzola and a fresh *mozzarella di bufala*, chased and captured
in the whey-filled bowl by the counterwoman's hand, then encased
in a small plastic bag. A few late purple-skinned figs, perhaps, or a
fat bunch of blue-black grapes, with just the right glossy sheen.

The figs, paired with a slice of *coppa*, would be perfect for
lunch along with a quick soup made from last night's leftovers.
The grapes for dessert. And for dinner, spaghetti doused with a
tomato sauce flavored with fresh basil, minced garlic, and olive
oil, all barely cooked so that the garlic's taste stayed light and
sweet. The pasta would be followed by thin scaloppine of pink
veal, cooked quickly with a big, fresh sage leaf and a small piece
of *prosciutto crudo* on top—so good they would fulfill the promise of their name, *saltimbocca alla romana*, and truly seem to
jump in one's mouth. A half-kilo of fresh *broccoletti*, their long,
skinny, bitter stems parboiled, then sautéed for a few moments
in hot olive oil, minced garlic, and a tiny, hot *peperoncino rosso*.

A small salad of tossed greens. A fat pear for dessert, with more of those blue-black grapes.

Those few moments of marketing, in the early quiet of my Roman mornings, were the only moments of semi-normality I lived during those weeks and months after we moved back to Rome. Greeting the people who sold us our food, talking with them about what looked best, were my daily attempts to live like other people, to live a normal life as I always had. The tomatoes and broccoli; the baby artichokes and spinach; the mozzarella and scaloppine they sold me; everything I carried home, cooked, served, then ate three times a day at the tiny oak table in our dining room became my lifeline to normality. For even though John could not talk, he could eat, and the two of us—somehow—managed to eat most of our meals in a silence that was at least companionable. For the entire year we were there, those quiet meals at our narrow oak table were a thrice-daily truce. Not once did John experience an anxiety attack at table. Not once did he sob. Silent tears never ran down his cheeks. And once his doctor discontinued the medications that weren't helping anyway, his digestion and appetite returned to normal. He may not have been able to talk at table, but neither did he act out his troubles. It all reminded me of his convalescence in Munich, when the doctor ordered him to eat so that his body would have the power to heal. It reminded me of my childhood illnesses, when after a week in bed I had suddenly gotten back my appetite and couldn't wait to eat.

An hour after one of our mealtime truces, I might be back to spitting bullets or sinking into a funk of my own, or listening, panicked as ever, to John banging his head against our iron bedstead. But each of those companionable, if silent, meals we ate together helped keep us both in the same quiet if rocky orbit, instead of shooting us willy-nilly into the blackness of inner space.

Each morning I would plan our day's three meals by what appealed to me in the market. I rarely made a list, just searched the stalls for what looked best. I would slip the bags of produce, meat, bread, and dairy products over my arms and head home. I would pause every morning in Piazza Farnese to push open the heavy door of Santa Brigida and kneel in the tiny chapel whose nuns chanted the holy hours at various times of the day.

The chapel, with its flickering candles, was almost never empty, and I found myself drawn to it each morning, especially to the painting of a Madonna and Child on one of the side walls. The Madonna, serene and smiling—guilelessly, happily—at the babe in her arms, always seemed to calm my nerves. I never knew exactly why. It may have been because I would unconsciously become the child when I walked into the chapel and basked in the gaze of the mother who could smile serenely and guilelessly and happily at me. Or it may have been because I was looking for instruction on how to smile myself, serenely and guilelessly and happily, at the child I had never managed to have. Whatever the reason, I always left Santa Brigida with enough strength to go back home for another day.

On the very worst days, when John had had an exceptionally bad afternoon or night or week, I might go into the chapel for days in a row and simply kneel there, my bags in a heap at my feet, tears running down my cheeks. On those days I would sometimes find to my horror that I was not only crying but pounding my fist on the back of the pew in front of me.

Ironically, as the months rolled by and John remained danger-ously ill, the banging of my fist on that pew slowly brought home the idea that it was not enough for John to see his doctor three times a week. I too needed help for myself, and could no longer stay—like the child I had been—waiting for my mother or hus-band to get better while I watched. I began to understand that I had to help force the issue or we both risked going under.

The truth is, the period of John's depression was more terrify-ing for me than when John was lying in the hospital in Roma-nia, worse than when he was unconscious and nearly dead in the intensive-care unit in Munich. During those early days after the shooting, the John who was lying there physically wounded was still the John I had met and gotten to know, the John with whom I had fallen in love, the John whom I had married. But after all these months of depression, the John with whom I was living did not just seem a total stranger, he *was* a total stranger, caught in a vise of darkness so crippling that I did not understand whether I could or should imagine a future with him alive or dead.

It all came to a head one day on one of our occasional walks together through the city. Usually John would spend a part of every day alone, simply walking the streets of Rome's historic center. At the beginning John's walks were often just for the sake of motion, putting one foot in front of the other, often blindly, just to help make the sun go down faster, so that he could take his next round of medications and return to the oblivion of sleep.

But on this particular day, we were out on the streets together, and for whatever reason, I fell behind him on our path across the Piazza Trilussa in Trastevere, a neighborhood just across the Tiber from our apartment on the Via Giulia. I watched him, just ahead of me, walking like a stick figure, rigid, tense, knees locked, rocking from side to side as he made his way slowly across the piazza in front of me. And for the first time since he had fallen ill, I felt not a whit of pity or sorrow but only pure, murderous anger. Anger not just toward his illness or our circumstances but fully and directly toward him, for letting his illness utterly hijack our life.

Before I knew it, I had become the madman, and found myself howling at him at the top of my lungs in the middle of the piazza, screaming and crying that if he didn't stop walking like Frankenstein that very instant, everything would be over between us very soon.

John—fittingly, perhaps—has no recollection whatever of this scene in Piazza Trilussa. But I remember it vividly—the moment when, for me, at least, the logjam was broken; the moment when I stopped waiting for him to get better and simply started trying to live again, as normally as one can during the unearthly, erratic abnormality that passes for everyday life during a family's imprisonment in depression.

14 ❧ Pears

Until he was about to turn ninety, my mother's father, Tony, rarely talked about Italy, the place from which his family had fled. Tony's Italy, when he mentioned it at all, meant a few scrawny goats—too few to feed a family—foraging on the steep, rocky hillsides of a poor village near Naples. Pressed to explain, Tony always demurred with a smile but in a tone that brooked no further questions: "It's better here, doll."

So when Tony told his two daughters that he wanted to celebrate his ninetieth birthday with a roast kid, cooked whole in a pit in the backyard "like in the old days," they were understandably flummoxed, for no pits had ever been dug in the backyards of their childhood, no goats ever roasted. My mother and aunt never understood their father's last big *wool-eee*, an old man's attempt to revisit the childhood he had shut off, the secrets and shames of his family's hard life on both sides of the Atlantic.

My mother's family never talked about these secrets openly, but instead let slip whispers: how Tony's big brother, Pete, had lost most of his toes to burns as he slept near a campfire while tending the family's tiny flock one bitterly cold night; how their mother died young, shortly after they emigrated; how their new stepmother fed them only what was left after her own children had eaten; how my grandmother Jennie's good-hearted cousins, the Romanos, used to slip the brothers food from their tiny grocery, basically keeping them alive. I've always wondered how much of a role gratitude played in Tony's decision to ask my grandmother to marry him, when she was only fifteen; I'll always wonder what provoked Tony's own descent into depression when he was already the father of two. All that has filtered down through the family's web of secrets was that he was unable to work for a couple of years, and that my grandmother, Jennie, took a factory job to keep the family solvent.

The only pleasant memory of Italy that Tony passed down to us came when he was in his nineties. It was, of all things, the memory of the pears of his youth. I never thought to ask him if the pears he remembered came from his family's own tree or from some wealthy landowner's nearby orchard. For all I know, Tony's memory of giant Italian pears may have come from a glimpse of a fruit vendor as the family passed a Neapolitan street market en route to the harbor from which their boat would leave for l'America.

For whatever reason, Tony's memory of pears—"This big!" he

would say, gesturing with his hands each time he spoke about them—struck a chord deep within me. Until I moved to Italy, I assumed he was dreaming an old man's dream when he spoke of those pears, that no pears on earth could ever be as big or juicy or richly flavored as the pears of his memory.

I was thirty-two when I first moved to Rome, and Tony, who outlived my grandmother by three days short of a year, had been dead for just a few months. It was early August when I moved, and the first fruits of that season's pear harvest were just coming into the city's string of neighborhood outdoor markets when I arrived. I hadn't thought about Tony's mythical pears for ages, until early one morning, at my tiny outdoor market near the Trevi Fountain, I stumbled across a wooden flat of pears so enormous, so perfectly greeny gold, that I could suddenly see Tony's plump, white hands moving in my mind, hear his gentle voice saying, once again, "This big!"

I bought a half-dozen of them, as if to confirm my grandfather's memory. I climbed the five flights of steep stairs to my tiny flat, then chose the biggest and ripest of the lot and placed it on one of my landlady's small white salad plates. I grabbed a small, sharp fruit knife and walked out to my back terrace, which overlooked a single, tall palm tree sheltered amid a warren of ochre-colored walls. I put the plate down on the table and realized with a start that Tony's memories had not been playing tricks on him. That pear was, in fact, "this big!"—plenty long to extend beyond the plate in each direction.

Tears suddenly started to roll down my cheeks, as Tony's voice and gesturing hands came back to life. Grief, which knows how to hide, and where, and for just how long, stopped hiding that morning. My grandmother Jennie had died a month after I moved to Europe, "of a broken heart when you left," my mother had told me hurriedly over the phone, a week after Jennie's death, after the wake and funeral mass, after the burial, after the family and friends had left. My mother, I felt keenly, was drawing blood to punish me for my flight, keeping my grandmother's death a secret until she was already buried.

Tony lasted 362 days longer, spending more and more of his afternoons and evenings at my parents' house, napping in his favorite chair by the window that overlooked Ash Creek. I never knew about the first funeral, and though my mother did not keep the news of my grandfather's death a secret, she did not want me to fly home for the second. Sitting on my little terrace in Rome, smelling my roses and jasmine and looking at the neighborhood's tall, sheltered date palm, I cut Tony's mythical pear into quarters, peeled it, cut out the seeds. Tears still running down my cheeks, I conducted my own private funeral and said good-bye to them both.

It was nearly a year after John's depression had emerged in full force that I exploded in anger in the Piazza Trilussa, raging against his Frankenstein walk. After the explosion, I called his doctor and told him John was not the only one who needed to talk. I wanted some answers myself by that time, and at bottom needed to know if I was part of the problem, for by then I had begun thinking that if I was, then maybe it was time to bolt. The doctor assured me that John believed I was part of the solution, and suggested I meet with him and his colleague, a family therapist. By the next week, not only was John seeing the doctor his usual three times a week, but I was seeing the family therapist once a week, and both John and I were meeting the doctor and family therapist yet another day each week.

Both specialists suggested that what they referred to as my unnatural patience with John's illness was perhaps contributing to its length, a notion I had never entertained. Until that time I had been terrified that any voicing of my complaints to John might push him over the edge, to irredeemable madness or suicide. It was, I think now, a childlike reaction, a feeling of being powerless and trapped. As a child I had never even known my mother had been desperately ill for months at a time; as a child I never would have thought I might be able to do something to make her better. My parents' failure to discuss her illness openly was not unusual, given the times, but it led me to think that there was nothing I could do except wait till the storm passed. Both doctors helped me begin to understand that it was not only natural to feel angry and impatient, but of enormous importance that I start demanding that John show me some signs of progress.

My anger had been quietly building over the months of John's sickness, but I became aware of it only toward the end of our

stay in Trevignano, when I drove into Rome one afternoon to
talk with an old reporter friend who also happened to be a Sister of Mercy. Sister Mary Ann Walsh was back in Rome on a
visit, and we met at the U.S. seminary on the Gianicolo, a hill
lined with umbrella pines and live oaks whose eastern end looks
over St. Peter's Square. I remember talking incessantly to her,
describing all that had happened, and being surprised myself
at the angry subtext of it all. I don't remember what Mary Ann
said that day after listening to my tale but I still have the letter
she wrote soon after, in which she talked about the suicide of a
beloved aunt, who, like my mother, had drowned herself in old
age. She suggested I might not be praying right, and explained
that at times she would get "t-eed-off with God and point out
that He (or She) is the Almighty One—I'm not—so it's about
time He (or She) did a little more for me. God's big enough
to hear and respond to our demands," she wrote. "Tell God in
strong terms what you're feeling."

I must have needed additional advice, though, because after
moving back to Rome, I talked about this idea with a Jesuit
friend before trying it out. John Navone listened to my explanation of Sister Mary Ann's advice and thought only a moment
before telling me he thought it was absolutely sound. "Anger is
about the only authentic voice I can imagine you having at this
point," he said. My pew pounding started just a few weeks later,
as if I had needed permission from both a nun and a priest to
feel and communicate the anger that was undeniably there.

A few months later, in one of those peculiar coincidences that some people would describe as grace, others as luck, my sister-in-law, Chan, sent me a *Washington Post* article describing a friendship that had sprung up between a Benedictine nun living in a Connecticut monastery and a Jewish writer who lived in California. The writer, Rhoda Blecker, described how, at a particularly low moment in her life, she had begun trying to pray, an attempt she said took the form of "yelling at God."

Pounding a pew sounded remarkably similar to yelling at God, and intrigued me enough that I filed the article away. I knew I wanted to write to these two women but I had no idea what I wanted to say. Months later, just before Christmas 1993, I wrote instead to St. Joseph's Abbey in Spencer, Massachusetts, where John had spent those four years between high school and college as a Trappist. In a short, dense note I described the troubles of our last few years and asked the monks to remember John in their prayers. Dom Augustine Roberts, the abbot, replied that John was still well remembered at Spencer and that my letter had been made available for the monks to read. He assured us that the monks were praying for us both.

Two weeks later, I finally managed to compose a long letter to Mother Miriam, the Benedictine portrayed in the *Washington Post* article. I described our situation in detail, Sister Mary Ann's advice on praying, and my Jesuit friend's concurrence. I described to Mother Miriam how I had taken to banging my fist on the back of the pew in front of me whenever I went into the little church of Santa Brigida. Although I never got noisier than that, I described myself as yelling, albeit silently, at God, telling him I had had more than my share during the last few years, that he had been pushing me around too hard and too long, and "*Basta!*" or "Enough already."

When I finished my letter, I walked up the Aventine Hill to the church of San Anselmo, the Benedictine headquarters in Rome, and told the black-robed doorkeeper I was looking for a Mother Miriam who lived in a Benedictine abbey somewhere in Connecticut. He quickly found a fax number and the address, the Abbey of Regina Laudis in Bethlehem, Connecticut. Back home, I decided to try the fax. The next morning our phone rang and a woman's voice, warm and full of joy, asked to speak to me. It was Mother Miriam, speaking on a line that had none of the usual hissing and buzzing of transatlantic calls in those days. When I asked where she was, she laughed and said not as far as I had thought, that for the past three years she had been living in Italy, just south of the great abbey of Monte Cassino, trying to reestablish an eighth-century monastery that had been burned and sacked by the Saracens in the ninth century and slid into an 1,100-year decline.

She said her old abbey in Connecticut had received my fax and faxed it on to her, and she had decided to phone immediately. Her unexpected call and the news that she was only a couple hours' drive south of Rome seemed unreal. I confessed to feeling as if I had gotten caught up in an episode of *The Twilight*

Zone, that 1960s television show that celebrated the paranormal and the bizarre. She laughed, a great pealing bell of a laugh, and asked me to come, for were we not meant to meet?

Two months later we did, at the abbey of San Vincenzo al Volturno, where a handful of Benedictine nuns still spend their days and nights in an unceasing round of prayer and work according to the sixth-century rule of Saint Benedict. The nuns worked like farmhands when they weren't chanting the Holy Office or helping a group of British archaeologists dig through the ruins of what was once one of the biggest and richest monasteries in Italy. The monastery's lands once stretched from sea to sea across the entire middle of the Italian boot; its 1,000 monks inhabited what was in fact a monastic city of extraordinary beauty on a high plateau in Italy's still wild and largely unsettled Abruzzi Mountains.

That weekend at San Vincenzo was a moment of calm and rest for both John and me. Rome and our desperately complicated life seemed at the other end of the earth during our short stay. Mother Miriam neither preached nor played Pollyanna nor uttered pieties during the brief interludes when she and I would have a moment to talk. Instead, the afternoon before John and I left, she and I took a walk together inside the monastery walls. She simply encouraged me to continue down what was obviously a very difficult road, not to despair along the way, and to keep to that path until I found where I was meant to be.

Written down, it may not seem like much. But her words

proved extraordinarily useful. Still, it may have been more her joy-filled presence that helped me most. To see someone so obviously full of joy about her rugged and simple medieval life— growing food; tending chickens; mucking out the barns; making cheese, wine, olive oil; cooking; and punctuating each day, which began at five a.m., with the chanting of the hours—reminded me that somewhere along the road of my own life I had lost not only the capacity for joy, but even the idea that joy still existed.

Although my memories of finally being able to yell at God while pounding the back of a pew in Santa Brigida have always been with me, I had, until writing this book, forgotten one of the most vivid and frightening telephone conversations I had had with my mother a short time before her death. The call occurred a few days after she had been put on a medication that her doctor hoped would help her from sinking further. Instead, it seemed that the pills pushed her over the edge.

My mother was barely able to speak that day on the phone, but she told me that when she tried to fall asleep at night, the faces of all the members of her family who had died had started appearing to her. They were speaking to her as well, she said. And they were beckoning. My mother, who always prayed on her knees every night before she went to bed, then confessed that there was something worse. In a voice full of terror and dread, she said she could no longer say her nightly prayers. Instead, when she looked at the crucifix on the wall, her entire being seemed to erupt in a silent howl, the epithet that she had muttered incessantly during her first depression that erupted at my birth: "sonofabitch." She was horrified at what she believed was blasphemy, and terrified of the consequences.

At the time, on a crackly phone line from Berlin, I did not hesitate a moment to tell her that her God on his cross would understand her cry, recognize her illness, not hold her accountable, not damn her to hell. But she simply could not believe me. Only now does it make sense to me why I, too, had been frozen in an overly patient silence during the endless months of John's depression, why I had not been able to pray in the only voice I had in those days, angry and fed up with the litany of woes that had come our way. My mother had yelled at God, and ended up a few nights later in the bitterly cold waters of a Connecticut salt marsh. She had been too ill to hear her words as a prayer, too ill to feel the grace that was there. It is only now, years later, that I can again see the grace that was waiting to catch her, the same grace that happened to catch me in time, a few lines of a letter from an old friend, a Sister of Mercy; a few words of concurrence from another old friend, a Jesuit professor; a few words of support from a new friend, a Benedictine from Connecticut who, like me, had ended up with an unexpected new life in Italy.

Our quiet weekend at San Vincenzo was a turning point for me. Not that I knew it then, but when I look back, I realize that although John remained deeply depressed and anxious,

PAULA BUTTURINI

still prone to bouts of weeping or shaken by repeated anxiety attacks, I could see that he was no longer as utterly mad as he had been even a few weeks earlier. That he had felt strong enough to come with me to San Vincenzo, that he had been able to enjoy our exploration of the archaeological ruins coming to light in the dig, meant he had already begun to turn the corner.

His doctor had long been encouraging him to do things that brought him pleasure, and by springtime John had doubled his walks about Rome, heading out rain or shine, with guidebooks or without, searching out ancient Roman architectural remains, medieval churches, views, museums, historic palazzi, losing himself in the city's past glories. We began pushing ourselves out after supper, not only for our usual walks but for free concerts in the city's baroque churches or for the occasional upbeat, tension-free movie. Listening to chamber music in the peaceful silence of an old cloister, where one need only look up to see the stars, gave our weeks a loose schedule; time no longer yawned endlessly before our eyes. Days no longer seemed to last a week, weeks no longer seemed to last a month.

I continued to cook and we continued to eat three meals a day together, and as John's depression began showing signs of lifting, we found we could occasionally even invite a very close friend or two over to share a meal with us without John falling into a panic of fear. When September rolled around, after we had been in Rome for nearly a year, we went up to Trevignano for a weekend visit to the Natansons. It was chestnut season already, and the tall chestnut trees that lined the rutted car track to their gate were having a bumper crop. The weekend happened to coincide with their daughter Phoebe's birthday, and John suddenly decided it was the moment for him to contribute to her birthday meal. I helped him gather a large basket of chestnuts, then watched as he cut crosses into their tough inner shells and boiled them in milk until they were tender and mealy. He showed us how to help peel the inner skin off, for it is one of those tedious processes that require many hands, and then he put them through a ricer and beat in powdered sugar, finally mounding the chestnuts into a mountainous shape on a large platter. This he covered with freshly whipped cream, to make it look like the snow-capped peak that gives it its name, Monte Bianco. Nobody said anything, for fear perhaps of breaking the spell, but I knew it was the first time in a couple of years that John himself had cooked anything, the first time he was truly able to come out of his misery and do something for somebody else. It was one more sign, the biggest one yet, that his depression was beginning to lift.

But it was by no means a straight, steady path back up to the light. Although that first year back in Rome seemed at the time to have lasted a decade, it was suddenly nearly over, our lease up for renewal. A close friend had a small, furnished apartment coming open about the same time, and we decided to put the horrors of the year in the Via Giulia apartment behind us. In October we would move into our friend Karen's sunny, light-filled apartment whose French doors provided a stunning view of the Colosseum in a section of Rome near the Forum that neither of us knew very well.

On paper it looked like a good plan. But we still did not realize the extent that even the tiniest change in routine or surroundings can terrify a person suffering from depression. And a move, even just across town, is no small change. John panicked as the move approached, and for the first few weeks in our new home, could barely speak from fear. His overreaction terrified me once more, and for the first few weeks, each time he went out for his daily walk I feared I would not see him alive again.

By Christmas, though, John began to accustom himself to the new apartment, its golden light, and the uninhibited view of the Colosseum, which loomed just outside our western windows. Slowly, our new surroundings in the heart of ancient Rome began to win him over. Once we began exploring the new neighborhood methodically, we fell in love with Rome a second time. I remember the day the two of us finally managed to get into Santo Stefano Rotondo, the oldest and one of the very few circular churches in Rome, which, at the time, was rarely open. The church, famous for its circular concentric naves, stands on the Celian Hill, which rose just behind our new flat.

We happened to arrive at a moment when fierce morning sunshine was pouring through the church's high clerestory windows.

The light was falling in Jacob's ladders into the otherwise dark interior, casting a luminescent glow on the two rings of ancient columns that give the church its circular shape. It was the stark interplay of light and dark that captivated John and me on that visit, and I can still picture us standing companionably next to each other and staring at the strong shaft of light that fell on one of a pair of massive Corinthian columns in the inner nave. I can still see the spiky stone acanthus leaves carved into that column's capital, and I remember trying to hold in my mind the light that was playing on them so that I might again have access to the light and peace the sunshine seemed to be giving off.

Acanthus grows everywhere in that corner of Rome, filling in the empty spots between more modern shrubs and trees, and its giant, shiny, spiky green leaves were a special comfort in winter, when many other plants were bare. The Greeks first carved acanthus leaves into the capitals of their columns, and the Romans copied the Greeks. To see acanthus growing live under the Corinthian columns where it was carved was one of those special gifts where the ancients speak to those of us living thousands of years later. John, who had spent more than twenty years studying and teaching Latin, redoubled his explorations of our new neighborhood after that visit. As the weeks passed, he found that he was no longer just putting one foot in front of the other to pass the time during his long, doctor-free afternoons; slowly, imperceptibly, he once again began to see what he was walking past and even take pleasure in what he saw.

Our new apartment near the Colosseum had a tiny kitchen carved out of and open to the living-dining room, and one could cook and entertain conversations at the same time. It was a big improvement over our former apartment, where the kitchen felt isolated, away from the life of the house, a room for a servant instead of a family. As John slowly gained strength, we found we could increasingly invite small groups of close friends over to share a meal with us, to drink a glass or two of wine, to talk, to listen, to take pleasure in the company of old friends.

As the year passed, the children continued spending half of their regular, seasonal vacations with us. The four of us would sit around the big wooden dining table, the Colosseum looking down upon us. After a meal, we would try to explain to Peter and Anna the course of their father's illness, to try to reassure them that he was beginning to feel more like himself, that the worst seemed to be over. How we searched—mainly in vain, it seems now—for words, phrases, explanations! I remember those attempts to explain and demystify Daddy's sickness, the children panicked in some ways, desperate for information on one level but just as desperate for silence, an understandable but vain hope that not talking about it might make the nightmare go away or, better yet, evaporate with neither trace nor memory.

Peter, in his late teens, seemed to seize up whenever we began to talk about John's illness, trying not to react or overreact, afraid perhaps to feel too much. Anna, six years younger, inevitably would cry, big tears spilling out of her blue eyes in neat tracks down her round cheeks. Even when our message was good— that the worst of the depression seemed to be behind him— Anna could only smile and sob at the same time.

When I look back, I don't remember either Peter or Anna asking many questions about their father's illness; in fact, our discussions—which we tried to focus on John's progress— seemed only in the short term to make them feel more distressed. We talked about it anyway, though we took care never to dwell on the lowest points of John's illness, sensing that they couldn't take it and didn't need to hear it. Since they spent half their vacations with us, rather than living full-time with us, their absence distanced them from the concrete horrors of day-to-day life with a person suffering from depression. But that distance also had its negative aspects; one tends to be more afraid of unknown terrors than the everyday terrors one can grow used to.

We knew that firsthand from Anna's initial reaction to John's shooting, when she was eight, and she and Peter visited John in the hospital for the first time. Anna laughed and chattered that day, completely tearless, clearly happy to see him. We thought she was simply too young to have recognized the gravity of the situation. We were thick-headedly wrong. For the following autumn, when Christmas decorations started going up in Germany, Anna became convinced that her mother was going to die during the holidays. Her mother, John, Peter, and I tried to ease her fears but Anna could find no comfort. All the terrors of the previous Christmas—too powerful for her even to voice at eight years old—simply returned, that much stronger for having been festering underground for an entire year.

When the worst of John's illness had begun to pass and he had just started to try to work again, Anna came alone on a weeklong visit. John told her about the old sketchbooks he had filled during his first trip to Europe at age twenty-three, when instead of taking photographs as souvenirs he had made sketches. He and Anna decided to buy new sketchbooks so that they could try their hand at a new series of drawings. One warm, sunny afternoon, the three of us took a long walk on the Oppio, another of Rome's ancient hills, which faced the front door of our apartment. There they began sketching the apse of the Baths of Trajan. Anna was disappointed with her results, which, next to John's, looked flat and childlike. When he suggested she alter a few key lines, making her straight horizontals into curves, Anna needed only an eraser and a few crucial changes to turn her flat sketch into a drawing with deep perspective, something that amazed us all. I cannot remember who was more proud that day, the father or his thirteen-year-old daughter.

I remember the first six months after we moved back to Rome from Trevignano—throughout the city's long, languid autumn and its short, sharp, sun-filled winter—when John's depression seemed utterly intractable. Sometime late in the long, damp spring that followed, just before the endless searing heat of the Roman summer had begun, the real John seemed to reawaken. The healing came in infinitesimal steps that never once resembled a smooth, upward path. It was always a jerky, tentative stop-and-go, a two-steps-forward, one-step-back sort of motion. The slightest change, glance, or comment could send John crashing and burning anew. But as spring turned to summer, I began to see that the dark hole he had been inhabiting was neither as deep nor as black as it had been, that while he often still looked terrified, he looked less terrified than before. It may have been that my own perspective was changing as well; I may have finally been able to see less terror in John because some of my own terror was beginning to fade.

And I remember that cool, sunny spring morning about two years into John's depression when I realized it had been a couple of weeks since I had had a vision of coming upon his lifeless body. Later, I realized that I no longer felt so entrapped by his moods, that I was no longer a hostage to his illness. John's silences began to melt away, and one day I was in the kitchen when I heard him laugh while reading a book. It was a tentative laugh, but a laugh nonetheless, and the first I had heard from him in what seemed like forever. I nearly cried at the sound of it.

During the worst of the illness we occasionally happened upon doctors who tried to make us believe that in these days of ever-improving medicines, one just has to experiment long enough to find the right drug or combination of drugs to put depression to flight. Perhaps for those comparatively lucky sufferers of drug-responsive depression, they might be right. But these were the same doctors who failed to mention that perhaps half the cases of stubborn, long-term depression they see are drug-resistant depressions, and that for those patients, no single drug or combination of drugs will work any magic at all. For these sufferers, the answer might lie in electroconvulsive therapy or in the simple passage of time needed for the chemicals gone awry in the brain to reverse themselves and return to their more usual state. The trick in that case is to keep the patient from killing himself while the healing inches forward.

John, with the help of a gifted doctor in Rome, a remarkably understanding editor and publisher in New York, a similarly patient bureau chief in Rome, and the fiercest personal determination to hang on to his life at all costs, managed the trick when his depression erupted about thirty months after the shooting. Like anybody living with depression, John was nothing short of heroic. But I know that it was also grace—not luck—and the strength of hope and prayer and anger and fear and love that brought him through.

15 ❧ Polenta

I remember the first time my father ever made us polenta, the yellow cornmeal mush that was basically his parents' daily bread back in the farm villages near Verona, where they had been born. My father used coarse-grained polenta, the old-fashioned kind that takes forty minutes to cook, and he stood at the stove, incessantly stirring the bubbling yellow mass with a tall wooden spoon for what seemed to my ravenous ten-year-old self like hours.

My mother was simmering a pot of her favorite stew, what she always called Lamb Marky, braised chunks of lamb shoulder *alla marchigiana*. Its rich sauce, strongly flavored with minced rosemary and garlic, dry white wine, and tomatoes, simmered long enough with the meat to turn it a dark, russet brown. We had always eaten it with potatoes till that night, but I guess my father had gotten a sudden *wool-eee* for polenta, which, back then, was strictly a northern Italian peasant dish, a cheap, nutritious filler like pasta, potatoes, rice, or grits and utterly unknown to my mother's southern Italian family.

When polenta begins to cook, it looks like yellow sand roiling about in boiling water. Only after much stirring and cooking over a slow flame does it finally thicken and pull away from the sides of the pan into a solid mass, a signal that it is nearly done. My father tipped the pot upside down over a cutting board, and like magic a steaming, yellow moon of polenta appeared. Like his mother, my father sliced it not with a knife, which would stick and tear the moist, grainy mass, but with a length of stout white thread, held taut like dental floss. I watched, fascinated, as he slipped the thread under one edge of the big yellow moon, then used both hands to pull the tautened thread firmly upward, producing a perfectly cut slice that he plopped onto each of our plates. My mother, standing at the stove, took each plate in turn and ladled out her lamb stew, dribbling the dark, meaty sauce over the bright yellow polenta.

I had been starving since I got home from school and smelled her stew already at a lazy simmer. Nevertheless, when the four of us finally sat down, I tried to eat as slowly as possible. From my first bite I knew that I wanted that feast to go on and on, and strangely enough, it has, because I have never forgotten how absolutely extraordinary it tasted to all of us that cold autumn night. It may have stuck in my mind because I was so hungry; or because my brother and I had watched our parents, laughing and cooking together, in our warm kitchen; or perhaps because the two of them produced a meal so perfectly honest and tasty that I knew that it was destined to be eaten again and again. I start craving it each year as we move deeper into autumn, but the real proof of its success may be that my father, over ninety now, still occasionally makes it for tiny dinner parties with his closest friends.

It was no mere accident that John's family ate polenta too. Eating polenta was like a Masonic handshake or secret code that whispered we were part of a tiny tribe of unwashed northerners who, like the great tribe of unwashed southerners, all of them hungry or looking for a better life, had fled Italy late in the nineteenth and early twentieth centuries. That John's family in Jersey City used to sit around their kitchen table eating polenta (theirs usually smothered with a fricassee of chicken and dried porcini mushrooms) meant we shared a similar historical past. When we met, both of us thought that sharing a particular history—hard-pressed families seeking to make a new life in another world—would make sharing a future easier. Neither of us has ever thought otherwise.

As John's health began to return, both of us were more than ready to kick-start our official marriage, which had in a sense been freeze-framed first by a bullet and later by depression.

John was also beginning to feel strong enough to work. By the end of 1993, he had managed to write about a dozen articles for the paper; by 1994, working at a more normal pace, he had written about six times as many stories and had even begun to travel for occasional articles. At that point, John's editors in New York said he could stay in Rome indefinitely as the *Times'* roving European business writer. That meant we could get our goods out of storage and officially install ourselves in Rome.

The chance to be reunited with our books, music, furniture, and clothes, in storage for nearly three years, pushed John and me to move one last time in Rome, across the Tiber to Trastevere. It was a noisy, charming neighborhood of narrow, cobblestoned lanes that used to be filled with blue-collar families but was undergoing both gentrification and the loss of its traditional mom-and-pop stores. Today, most of the tiny vegetable and fruit shops, the dingy one-room groceries, the minuscule trattorie whose bills were figured on the paper tablecloths, have been replaced with tacky nightspots, bars, karaoke joints, and cheap pizzerias, the lot covered in graffiti that the city does not bother to erase.

We moved into a small apartment whose ceiling beams had been cut about the time the masts of the *Mayflower* had been felled, whose windows stretched nearly twelve feet high. The flat had no view, but was airy and light, and, lacking daylong direct sunlight, rarely felt like an oven, no small thing in a hot country that has yet to embrace air-conditioning. When we finally set up housekeeping after nearly three years of living in furnished flats, we were happy to be back to some sort of normality, but we also felt inundated by our belongings. Since both of us found it easier living pared down, I gave away boxes of kitchenware, clothes, books, records, and anything else we did not plan on using daily. My sense of isolation also diminished at this time, since John, feeling increasingly stronger, no longer feared the visits of friends and family. Within a couple of weeks, both of us felt we were settling into our new, old life: John working at the *Times* office, a ten-minute walk across the Tiber, and me writing from home.

Kick-starting our marriage meant more than just living once again amid our own belongings, more than just refinding each other after John's long illness. I was in my mid-forties already, John nine years older, and I knew that if we were ever going to have a child together, there was already little, if any, time left. Ironically, it was my relationship with John's Anna that had reawakened my old longing for a child of my own, a longing that I had been obliged to put aside repeatedly, when John was shot, when he got hepatitis, when he spiraled down, lost, into depression.

I had known Anna since she was five, and her openness toward me had always been a gift. I never played at being her mother, but I loved being around her and watching her mind and heart grow. Once when she was still very young she told me that she did not like the word *stepmother* because fairy-tale stepmothers were too mean. She tried to come up with a new, more neutral word to describe our relationship, and suggested that perhaps I could be her fa-wi, short for father's wife, while she could be my hu-da, short for husband's daughter. Even if her terms never caught on, the thoughts behind them took root. Over the years, she and Peter showed me repeatedly that the complicated relationship I had had with my mother did not necessarily mean I would provoke a similarly complicated relationship with all other small beings in the universe.

The idea of a child resurfaced shortly after we moved back to Rome and began our four-way meetings with John's doctor and family therapist. John, who already had two children, who was fighting to come out of a serious depression, who was still trying to get back to work on a regular basis, was understandably far more hesitant than I about the idea, though I also worried that it might be too big a gamble. Still, I think our doctors understood far better than either of us at the time that I was likely to feel cheated in our marriage at some point in the future if we did not at least agree to try. In the end, our decision to try to have a child was not an intellectual choice but a visceral one: a now-or-never decision.

In June of 1996, on the advice of our doctors in Rome, we flew to London to consult with a fertility expert whom John's doctor believed would be helpful to us both. It was our first weekend trip outside Italy in years, and we were excited at the thought of a weekend away together. The consultation was relaxed but to the

point. The doctor was aware of our ages and relieved that neither of us was interested in doing anything scientific to enhance
the utterly slim chances of a pregnancy (no drugs, no hormones,
no surgical or fertility procedures, not even so much as the daily
taking of my temperature). He told us simply that it was highly
unlikely I would become pregnant, but that there seemed to be
no physical impediments that would absolutely rule it out. That
was how we wanted it; either I would conceive naturally or I
would not. The trip to London was a balm: talking with the
fertility expert there made me understand almost immediately
that it was not so important that I become pregnant as it was
that I consciously tried to leave myself open to new life—to our
own as a couple, or to the possibility of a child. That John went
along with it, despite deep reservations, was, I think now, what
sealed our marriage vows, for I knew how much he was risking
to agree. Quietly, then, I started hoping for a girl.

If it was Anna and Peter who gave me the courage to consider
having a child; if it was John's psychiatrist who helped us for-
mulate the idea; if it was the London fertility expert who said it
was a possibility, however unlikely, it seemed to have been a big
family wedding back in Washington, D.C., that June that did
the trick. Rice was thrown in the direction of John's niece and
her groom. A few grains must have bounced off and come my
way, because a month or so after the celebrations, the doctors
told me later, I was pregnant.

Not that I had any idea at the time. It was not until late

September, two months later, when I made my ritual morning cup of tea that I noticed anything unusual. The tea, my usual English Breakfast, with milk, tasted metallic, bitter, nasty. I emptied it into the sink and made another in a different cup, thinking some soap residue might have contaminated the first. I sipped, and again that metallic, bitter taste filled my mouth. It was not until a few days later, still tea-less, that I realized I had missed my monthly cycle in August. I had thought little of it, because my gynecologist had been telling me for years that I seemed to be nearing menopause.

I told John my suspicion, but instead of floating on air, as I was, he blanched. The news clearly taxed his newfound equilibrium, and I soon felt as if I had been taken hostage again by his illness. I wasn't so much worried that the pregnancy would send him back into depression as I was angry that his depressive tendencies might continue to threaten or rule our life together forever. The years following our wedding had been all about what *he* needed, never about what I might need. Now, the two of us reverted to psychological form: John feeling guilty and frightened for not being able to dance me around the living room in celebration of the thought that I might be pregnant, I feeling murderous that his depressive tendencies might ruin the joy I felt at the thought of expecting a child.

Most of the fears I had had about having children dissipated after my mother's death. The joy I felt at becoming pregnant for the first time at forty-five seemed to erase the rest. This joy may have been partly fueled by psychological therapy, by the hormones that come with pregnancy, or by the idea that by being pregnant I was finally doing something that was not just about John or Peter or Anna but about me, my marriage, and our growing family. The joy I experienced was vivid, profound, and unchanging. I remember once at Sunday Mass thinking I had never truly understood the word *Alleluia* until I was deep into my pregnancy.

John had to work hard throughout those nine months to keep his fears at bay. And he did work incessantly with his doctor during this period to do just that, a decision I understood and appreciated. What made it easier was that I could understand his concerns, understand when he said that he did not want to be an old father, an exhausted father, a sick father. I could understand when he said he did not want Peter or Anna to feel sidelined by the birth of another child. I could understand when he said he found it terrifying to think that he was too fragile for the worry he knew he would feel about a delivery and birth. As disappointed as I was over his initial reaction, I also loved him for everything he did to overcome it. His doctor never let John's fears get the better of him, and we took the doctor's suggestion to do whatever it took to help John look forward to the birth rather than to fear it.

With that in mind, we traveled to northern Italy to visit Figino Serenza, the hamlet south of Lake Como where John's paternal ancestors had lived for generations. John is his family's unofficial historian, and we spent an entire weekend rooting around the basement libraries of local churches, eventually tracing the Tagliabue family's genealogy back to the mid-1700s. Whenever we weren't reading bound black church registries, we seemed to be eating long, delicious meals with John's many cousins, who still live in the area and run a highly successful wood-veneer business.

In a similar effort to put the shooting further behind him, John overrode his fears enough to return to Romania a couple of months before the baby's due date. He had an emotional meeting with Dr. Radulescu, the surgeon who had saved his life, and another poignant meeting with Georgina Stanea, the nursing administrator who had worked tirelessly to get Timişoara's airport open long enough for the Red Cross to fly John and me to safety. While in Timişoara, John learned the name of the man who had shot him, and though initially curious, he decided that meeting his assailant would accomplish nothing. John was in Romania to write a magazine article for the *Times* about Romania's future and our own. He was not there to settle old scores but to get beyond them, to look toward our future, not toward our past.

Throughout that fall, I kept my pregnancy secret from everyone but John and our doctors. At the end of the first trimester, in October, I told only my father, who I knew would be as thrilled as I was. But given my age, and my doctor's initial concerns, I decided it would be wiser to keep our secret until I was fairly sure the pregnancy was likely to continue to term. Since it was autumn, and Roman apartments are notoriously cold in winter, it was physically easy to hide it under a couple of layers of clothes.

It was not until Thanksgiving—a feast we always celebrated by inviting any solitary American we knew who was unlikely to cook a turkey dinner for themselves—that we went public. We called Peter and Anna, all our brothers, and our closest friends to tell them our news. It was the happiest, most thanks-filled Thanksgiving I ever experienced, and until that point the only time in my adult life that I was not full of worry about one thing or another.

Back in September, when my breakfast tea suddenly tasted bad, my gut had told me two things: that I was likely pregnant, and that the best way to make sure all went well was to relax and enjoy it. It helped that I had never been afraid of pregnancy itself. Given my mother's four bouts of postpartum psychosis, I was more concerned that problems might develop in the hormonal rush that occurs after birth, even though John's doctor told me repeatedly that my mother's problems did not in any way condemn me to have them, too.

It was during that first week of learning I was pregnant that I found myself deciding to try to keep even my concerns to the basics. Even if I was pregnant for the first time in my life at age forty-five, I was healthy, and in excellent shape. My mother had had her last child at forty; John's mother had had him at forty-four. In my mind and soul, I felt I was carrying either a perfectly healthy baby or a frog. I knew that no amount of worrying would change the latter into the former. I had never been very good at praying for specific things, and decided I could not simply start now. My prayer, daily and unending, was to put my usual worrying nature aside and enjoy the pregnancy. That said, I felt absolutely held aloft by the prayers of my friends, as well as by our Italian neighbors and acquaintances, who could not have shown more interest had I been a beloved daughter.

Is there any European country more theoretically disposed to loving children than Italy? And since Italians themselves pretty much stopped having babies in recent decades—Italy has one of the lowest birthrates in Europe—there was nothing they liked more than taking vicarious pleasure in someone else's pregnancy. Neighbors and shopkeepers on our old Trastevere street adopted me from the moment they learned I was pregnant. The elderly *barista* at the old café across the street from our flat, where I would buy our daily milk and occasionally drink an afternoon *spremuta d'arancia*, freshly squeezed orange juice, refused to accept payment the day he and his wife noticed I was expecting, and came out from behind the bar to shake hands and congratulate me properly.

Despite my obstetricians' serious concerns, my pregnancy was utterly uneventful, as was the birth, a cesarean that was anticipated from my first visit. We found a clinic that would allow the baby to remain with me twenty-four hours per day, and this being

Europe, where insurance companies do not overrule doctors, a cesarean meant I would be expected to remain hospitalized for at least a week. During the Christmas holidays, John, Peter, Anna, and I held a family powwow to come up with a name that would please us all. We asked the children to list all the names they liked, all the names they loathed. We discarded all their hated names, then in a series of eliminating votes, we came up with the one we all liked best. In the end, we all voted for Julia, a name that not only worked in many languages but that recalled John's paternal Aunt Julia, the aunt he felt closest to and who had lived above them in Jersey City when he was a boy.

We soon learned that the birth would likely occur during Anna's spring vacation, and she made plans to arrive in time to welcome her sister's arrival. Anna was the first family member besides me to see Julia, since John was making a phone call at the time she was brought down from the operating room to the nursery. John and Anna had a special week together, just the two of them, at the time of Julia's birth, and Anna, just sixteen, was able to talk at length about how the birth tore at her emotionally, making her both happy and sad. She was genuinely thrilled to hold Julia in her arms, genuinely sad to understand that it was Julia, not she, who would be living with their daddy full-time.

John told Anna that he could understand her conflicting feelings, but reminded her that she knew and had her daddy when he was still a young man, something that Julia would never be able to experience. "Do you remember when you were little and

you used to dive off my shoulders into the lake at Trevignano?"
John remembers asking her. "I wonder when Julia will be your
age whether I'll still be able to have the strength to have her
dive off my shoulders." John's words came from the experience
of his own childhood, the last child of four, whose parents were
a good deal older than those of his friends. John recalls growing
up with only an older man as a father; he recalls being jealous of
his two oldest brothers, eleven and seven years older, who knew
their father when he was young and vital.

It was just last summer, when John, Anna, Julia, and I were
at the French lake that has come to substitute for our old lake
in Trevignano, that John recalled this emotionally charged conversation with Anna after Julia's birth. He was in the water
with both girls when Julia asked to dive off his shoulders. She
did, several times. Then John suggested to Anna, a tall woman,
twenty-seven at the time, that she try diving off his shoulders as
well. Anna climbed up and dived, too, and when she came up
for air, John said to her, "Do you remember our conversation in
Rome?" When Anna assured him she did, he said, "Isn't it funny
that you're both able to jump off my shoulders? I guess I was
wrong back then."

That Anna, at age sixteen, could not only recognize but also
speak about the uneasy mix of joy and sadness she experienced
at Julia's birth, to her father and to me, helped all of us immeasurably. Had she not been able to voice her sadness, it might
have gone underground and blocked any happy tie between the

two girls, or damaged her ties to John. A decade later, Julia flatly adores both Peter and Anna, looks forward to their visits as much as we do, and mourns when they head back to Germany. Peter, who keeps Julia in the *Monty Python* reruns both of them love, is already trying to convince John and me that Julia will soon be old enough to make the four-hour train trip to Germany to visit him and Anna on her own, without us.

Eight days after Julia's birth, John saw Anna off at the airport, then came straight to the clinic to collect us. Even in the taxi on the way home, I could see that the powerful emotions of the week had affected him strongly. He was tense and noticeably quieter than he had been each time he and Anna together had come to visit. As afternoon turned to evening, his mood nose-dived. By nightfall he was barely able to speak, and I could see all the old symptoms of anxiety beginning to rise. It was the first time in some years I had seen John become so unhinged. I kept hoping he would be able to beat the symptoms back on his own, but by bedtime I knew he was losing the battle.

I called his doctor, who came to the flat at once and administered a sedative in hopes of braking John's downward slide. The doctor's arrival helped soothe me, too, for he took the time to admire the baby and remind me at length that birth, though easier to think about than death, is still a life-shaking event for anybody. The doctor's soft, reassuring voice helped calm me just as his sedative had already calmed John. Once the doctor left, the three of us soon fell asleep. As I drifted off, I kept thinking that this was not at all the sort of homecoming I had envisaged. I wish I could say that I knew at the time that John would come around, but all I really knew was that he looked about to go off the rails again. Even the hint of that set me sinking, and I felt even worse that I had been so focused on my own potential post-partum problems that I had not foreseen John's.

Throughout my pregnancy I had tried to avoid worrying, to simply let myself float along on a hormonal rush of well-being, physical and psychological. I hadn't focused at all on the possibility that John might panic when Julia finally arrived. I knew how happy Peter and Anna made John, and I did not know then that he had panicked briefly when each was born. I simply never focused on the possibility that Julia's appearance might panic him briefly as well. I felt stupid for being so blind, for not even entertaining the notion that John might not be all-embracing and joyful when we returned from the hospital. I felt cheated, too, as much for Julia as for myself.

Those first days at home after Julia's birth alternated from one moment to the next between pure joy and utter dread. The joy of finally seeing my firstborn's face, the dread that John's setback would lead back down the road from which he had struggled, that Julia's appearance in this world might somehow have to be traded for John's health and sanity. John's new anxieties terrified me for our future. As for the present, the rush of postpartum hormones was clearly keeping me off balance and disturbed; I could not read a newspaper without weeping, tears of joy over the slightest schmaltz-filled yarn, tears of unutterable sadness over just about everything else. I kept reminding myself to be thankful that, unlike my mother, I knew it was hormones—and not my sanity—that were in such a state of flux.

Over the next days and weeks, John worked even more closely than usual with his doctor to fight off the panic that occasionally rose within him, to master his irrational fears about whether he could be as good a father to Julia as he had been to Peter and Anna, about whether Julia's presence might somehow damage the ties he had to his firstborn children. That he did in fact learn to master those fears and reverse the slide—all the while continuing to work and live with a newborn and a forty-six-year-old new mother who was herself worried about postpartum blues—impresses me still. That over the next weeks he was able to fight off his panic and turn himself into the very same father I had seen with Peter and Anna—loving, nurturing, playful, wacky—made me realize our marriage was on the right track again at last. I felt my bolting days were over, that it would be near impossible for me to walk out on a man who had conquered such panic, a man with whom his youngest daughter was so utterly taken.

The journal I kept of Julia's early life is an old, tattered reporter's notebook I grabbed in such haste the day we got home from the clinic that I started writing in it from back to front.

The journal began as a simple feeding timetable, reminding me at what time I had last fed Julia and which breast she had emptied. At the time, my short-term memory seemed short-circuited, and I could not remember anything from one minute to the next. I had suffered this sensation once before in my life, during the first weeks of John's hospitalization after the shooting, when I had to write down everything anyone said to me, since my mind could not grab, record, or play back any conversation, no matter how important.

Julia's pediatrician, a young Italian mother with children of her own, was adamantly in favor of breast-feeding, and worked with Julia and me while we were still in the clinic to make sure things were progressing correctly. New mothers in Italy benefit from a midwife visit after they go home, a godsend for a first-time mother, who needs all the help she can get. I had read any number of books and pamphlets on breast-feeding before Julia was born, and all of them seemed hopelessly vague and romantic when faced with a squalling, starving infant who could not seem to latch on to a milk-engorged nipple. My brother once described breast-feeding as the most unnatural of natural acts, and until Julia and I finally got the routine down, I could not have agreed more.

All the books and pamphlets talked up breast-feeding's economies, how new parents did not have to pay the price of expensive baby formulas to feed their child. None of them seemed to mention that a breast-feeding mother's enormous appetite would more than make up for the difference. In those early days at home, I simply could not get enough food in my stomach to satisfy my hunger. And no matter how much I ate, the weight just kept falling off my bones.

For breakfast, I found myself eating eggs, potatoes, toast, fruit, yogurt, muesli, and the occasional bit of leftover meat. By ten a.m., starving again, I would down an enormous bowl of fresh ricotta, covered in tiny strawberries. By lunchtime I would be ravenous once more and would eat a bowl of pasta or a plate of risotto, followed by meat, a mound of cooked vegetables, a salad, and more bread than I had ever eaten in my life. Three hours and a nap later, I would be famished yet again and fix myself enormous slabs of Gorgonzola cheese on dark country bread. Once John got home, I would eat a supper as big as my lunch and follow it up with a few pieces of fruit.

John, who was cooking those first few days after my return from the hospital, could barely keep pace with my hunger. Even though Julia and I were growing stronger by the day, I hesitated to count on John to take up the slack, since he was still feeling overwhelmed after the birth, and I was simply too exhausted to buy and prepare all the food I needed to eat. We did not own a car, and there was no way to do food shopping except on foot, dragging one of those two-wheeled, old-lady shopping carts behind me. Although I could buy fresh pasta, bread, fruit, vegetables, and milk at nearby shops, the butcher was several blocks away, at the time too far for me to even consider. That second week out of the hospital, I was positively saved by Eleni, my Greek-American friend. Eleni, who had two children of her own, knocked on my door one morning when I was still too weak to be out of bed for long. When I opened the door, she was standing there with hampers of cooked food, all ready to be heated and served.

I can still taste Eleni's Italian mother-in-law's recipe for turkey breast poached until tender in milk, butter, and Parmigiano cheese, the creamy sauce flavored with bits of minced onion, carrot, and celery. I can still see Eleni's enormous roulade of beef, big as my arm, stuffed with ham, cheese, spinach, and herbs, and flavored by a carrot-rich tomato sauce. Eleni brought a vat of homemade mashed potatoes, Italian-style, enriched and lightened with nearly a quart of milk. She brought a big container of cooked zucchini, another of rice, another of beans. No one ever gave me a better gift in my life than that hamper of ready-to-eat meals; to this day I do not know how I would have survived that second week at home without Eleni's food. I suppose I might have eventually figured out a way to have one of our local trattorie deliver meals to our door, but by the time I had eaten my way through Eleni's bounty, I was strong enough to do the shopping and cooking myself.

Both Julia's pediatrician and my gynecologist discouraged me from switching to formula during two long bouts of mastitis. That meant breast-feeding every two hours for days at a time, while taking antibiotics. During the second bout, when Julia was about two months old, the gynecologist discovered I was on the verge of developing an abscess, which could mean hospitalization. "Julia needs her mother at home, not in the hospital," the doctor told me, asking when I had last fed her. When I answered, "Just now," the doctor did not hesitate: "Well, then, Julia has just had her last natural feed from you."

The doctor's advice took me utterly by surprise, and I walked out of her cramped basement office, huge tears spilling down my cheeks, for my hormones were still in an uproar, from the birth or the breast-feeding or both. I knew the doctor was right, but I had not expected her pronouncement to be so sudden or categorical. Still crying, I walked out of her office into the normal chaos, pedestrian and vehicular, of the Viale Trastevere, the neighborhood's biggest boulevard. I walked into our local pharmacy, tears still gushing, and handed one of the women behind the counter the doctor's prescription for Julia's formula and mine for shutting down my milk. This being Italy, the woman came out from behind the counter, handed me a pack of tissues, sat me down in a chair, and asked what was wrong. Still blubbering uncontrollably, I told her that my doctor had just decreed I could no longer breast-feed.

The entire shop—pharmacist, salesclerks, and elderly patrons alike—came to a momentary, silent standstill. Then, this being Italy, everybody in the shop started talking at once, offering comfort and advice and telling me not to be upset—that everything would be all right, that my baby would be fine, that I soon would be feeling like myself, that I should just take the pills as prescribed and go home and steal a long nap.

Group therapy over, I finally managed to stop crying, paid my bill, and walked the rest of the way home. I took a long nap, as suggested. At feeding time, I made up a bottle of formula and worried how Julia would react. Ravenous herself, Julia never missed a beat, and sucked on that plastic nipple until the bottle was drained. When she was through, I took my milk-stopping drug and prayed that the threatened abscess would be averted. During the coming days, my milk dried up as it was meant to and my hormones simmered down.

The elderly ladies in the pharmacy were correct. Everything was all right, my baby was fine, my husband was on the mend, and soon I was feeling like myself.

16 ❧ Cookbooks

$\mathcal{E}$very family has its creation story. Mine was always recounted by my mother, in just the same way, with the same tone of regret. When I married your father, she would always begin, I didn't know how to boil water. I couldn't make a soft-boiled egg. I didn't know how to make coffee, where to put it in the pot. If it hadn't been for your father teaching me how to do everything, we would have starved. I don't want you to grow up like I did, with my toast always buttered for me every morning. I want you to be able to do everything.

At some point after their wedding, years before I was born, Irma Rombauer's *Joy of Cooking* showed up in my parents' kitchen. It's still there, covered in the same neat brown paper bag cover that we always used to cover schoolbooks. Decades later my mother bought the updated version, written by the mother and her daughter, and she complained forever after that all the good recipes were gone, and the ones that remained were all wrong. "Oyma" was how my mother always referred to the book and its author. "What does Oyma have to say about it?" she would wonder aloud, and when I was very little, I always thought that my mother knew Oyma intimately, that she was perhaps an old childhood friend, someone who had moved away, who inexplicably never wrote at Christmas but who had left indelible traces behind in her thick, heavy cookbook filled with basic recipes like griddle cakes, dry dressing, or roast beef hash.

After Oyma, Adelle Davis began appearing in our kitchen with alarming frequency. *She*, for we were never on a first-name basis with her, had written one of the early health-food bibles, *Let's Cook It Right*, a 1947 book that much intrigued my father, as did *Let's Eat Right to Keep Fit*, a later volume. *She* was to blame for the whole-wheat-bread phase of my childhood, all those brown sandwiches I threw away at school after a bite or two out of the middle. *She* was responsible for tiger's milk, a nasty concoction of molasses and brewer's yeast. Her only saving grace, in my mind, was a recipe for pancakes made of potatoes, grated whole, skin included, and cooked very rapidly in a bit of very hot oil or fat, with a touch of raw onion thrown in toward the end. Everybody seems to love them still, despite their provenance.

Luckily James Beard, portly like my mother's father, appeared to save me from other early health-food enthusiasts (like D. C.

Jarvis, M.D., a Vermont folk doctor whose food credo centered around apple cider vinegar, which we sprinkled on everything from spinach to New England Boiled Dinner, and which we used diluted as a gargle and, mixed with honey, as a sleep tonic). We called him Jamesie, for reasons long lost, and we all own several of his cookbooks, filled with anecdotes that made us want to cook.

I can still taste Jamesie's beef Stroganoff, which cooked in moments and which my mother always served with rice and a healthy shower of chopped, fresh parsley. I still make his chicken sauté with white wine and herbs. I still love to serve his light, white-wine-and-chicken-soup version of French onion soup, always using Parmigiano instead of the standard Swiss cheese topping. Our French friends love Jamesie's Chocolate Roll, a fallen chocolate soufflé cooked flat on a cookie sheet and rolled, jelly roll–style, around a filling of freshly whipped cream. But as with all our favorite author-cooks, my family read Jamesie's books as much or more for the sheer pleasure of the read than because we were looking to try a new recipe or to find out what one actually did with salsify or parsnips or quince.

When I was turning seventeen, I asked my parents to give me Julia Child's landmark tome, *Mastering the Art of French Cooking*. Julia—we always warbled the *u* so it sounded more like "Juuuuulia"—was fun to watch on Boston's public television station, and nearly as fun to read. Her thick cookbook, all 684 pages of it, sought to demystify French food for American home cooks. I found it useful for facts and basics and methods, but in the end too full of butter and cream, too complicated and fussy for our family taste. Juuuuulia stayed the course anyway, and my father bought her last cookbook, *The Way to Cook*, in his late eighties, reading it avidly, even if he had begun to lose interest in actually producing her recipes for eating.

I was in my late twenties and already living in Texas when my mother drove to a fancy mall in Stamford, Connecticut, one afternoon to sit in on a cooking class given by Jamesie himself. She came home bubbling and talked for an hour on the phone about her wonderful afternoon. Better yet, Jamesie had, when asked, been able to recommend a new Italian cookbook, recently published, that was nothing like the standard red-sauce wonders that had defined Italian cooking in the United States up until that point.

The book was Marcella Hazan's *The Classic Italian Cookbook*, which eventually became the best-selling Italian cookbook in the United States. My mother bought two copies on the spot, one for herself and my father, and the other for me. We devoured Marcella's book and its recipes like no other cookbook before it, and Marcella in no time supplanted all others in our family pantheon of kitchen gods. "Marcella says . . ." became our creed.

I actually met Marcella in Dallas a couple of years later, when she gave a cooking class at a new Williams-Sonoma store, and I dutifully presented her with my heavily stained copy of her first book to autograph. Marcella was happily shocked to find I had a first edition of her book, which had sold badly under its original publisher. And she was touched to learn that our Jamesie, her friend and colleague, James Beard, had been quietly promoting her behind her back.

A few years later, after my move to Rome, I called Marcella to ask if I could interview her for a story for United Press International's feature wire while I was in Venice covering a medical conference. Wire service reporters often were forced to cover deadly boring stories, from taking dictation on the results of a Russian–Italian track meet to covering the summer visit of some Podunk mayor who had found his way to Europe. To have been invited into Marcella's Venetian kitchen, to have watched her cook up a lovely lunch for me, which she then served on her terrace, to have a couple of hours in which to talk food and drink with my family's favorite cook, in her own kitchen, more than made up for all the evenings of my life that I had spent with a heavy, black phone receiver scrunched between my neck and shoulder, and typing Russian names, letter by letter, hour after hour, from some beer-fueled sports stringer, "Medvedev, M for Mary, E for Edward, D for David, V for Victor . . ."

Julia's creation story, not surprisingly, also centers on food. Within a few weeks of her birth, John's postpartum crisis melted away more quickly than I ever would have expected. As summer approached, we could not wait for Peter and Anna's visit and Julia's introduction to Trevignano. John, for all his stated fears about reentering fatherhood, was already completely at ease around her and loved to sit with her on his shoulder, singing all the nursery songs he had sung to Peter and Anna when they were small. From her earliest days she visibly relaxed whenever she was nestled between his broad shoulder and slim neck.

About the time that Julia turned four months old, her pediatrician told me that she was ready to be introduced to solid food. In teaching Julia how to eat—which I felt was one of the most fundamental parts of teaching her how to live—I was bent on breaking the mother-daughter eating game my mother had started playing on and off soon after I was born. My mother used to say that when I was three or four I did not like to eat. Family lore says the only two things I gobbled down back then were homemade chicken soup with tiny stars of pastina, and black olives, the latter preferably eaten in tens, a pitted one stuck onto the tip of each finger.

My mother was certain it was her own bad eating habits that had caused her "nerves"; she did not want me to end up like she had: skinny, anxious, depressive. Convinced that food and a healthy appetite were the answer to mental and physical health, she took to feeding me a thick, dark brown viscous "tonic" twice a day for several months, before breakfast and supper. I still remember gagging it down until when I was about five that ugly brown bottle finally disappeared for good. My own healthy appetite and naturally fast metabolism—inherited from both my parents—must have kicked in at about that time, for my mother never felt the need to push food on me again until after I had left home for college.

Once I left, every phone call, every letter my mother ever wrote me, and she wrote unfailingly, hundreds of letters over the years, mentioned food in some guise or other. She would tell me about a dinner party she and my father had thrown, detailing each of the dishes they had made for their guests. She would send me new recipes she had discovered, old recipes I had requested. Many of her phone calls and letters, written in the rounded, Palmer-method hand of her school days, ended with the admonition, "Eat more, and pray." And every time I returned home—from college, from Texas, from England, from Spain, from Italy, Poland, or Germany—it was always the same: my mother eyeing me slowly from top to bottom, followed by the inevitable judgment, "Too skinny, you look like hell," even if I had not lost an ounce since I had last seen her.

From college onward, once I was out of the daily orbit of my mother's kitchen, pushing food on me became a bad habit she developed, a way to reassert the control over my life that she knew was slipping away. Meal after meal, year after year, in my late teens and early twenties, I declined to play her game. Ours was a tango I most definitely did not want to pass on to my own daughter. Force-feeding might work for geese, I thought, but not for children. I wanted mealtimes without the background music of a mother's voice, wheedling or insisting, "More? Just a little. A mouthful. Can't you finish this last bit?"

At the same time, though, I wanted Julia to enjoy her food the way John's family and mine all did, to like most foods, to enjoy trying new things, to approach a table three times a day with a sense of pleasure. "Don't smell it, eat it!" was the standard line John's father would use whenever any of his four boys exhibited the slightest sign of turning picky at table. His mother's version of that same line, "Food is not meant to be smelled, it's meant to be eaten," also warded off potentially finicky behavior. To this day there is almost no food these four brothers don't enjoy.

Similarly, I wanted to encourage Julia, as my mother had encouraged me, to listen to her stomach, and to think about what it was her body might "need" to eat. I wanted her to understand *wool-eees* and I wanted her to respect them. Both John and I grew up eating the food our parents made for the family as a whole, and neither of us believed that children's food should be different from adult food; once she got physically old enough to eat anything, I wanted Julia to eat what we ate night after night. I was not about to overturn our eating habits for Julia, nor was I planning a second career of making special meals on demand. I wanted Julia to climb aboard our family's established food wagon, not hitch our wagon to hers.

I expect every country has its own prescribed method of weaning. Italy, which keeps to its historical food traditions perhaps more than most developed nations, certainly had a straightforward, step-by-step system for how and when to introduce solid foods to babies, never before four months. I still have the typed single sheet of feeding instructions, titled "The Stages of Weaning," which the pediatrician gave me as Julia approached that four-month milestone.

The pediatrician suggested mashing a single slice of banana to see whether she was ready to move beyond formula. From her eagerness to eat that first spoonful of banana, given in the warm morning sunshine of our wisteria-covered terrace in Trevignano, it was clear Julia was more than ready. But the doctor warned me that I must never introduce another new food until the baby had eaten the first one—and showed no ill effects from it—three days running. The slow addition of new foods, the doctor said, meant that potential allergies could be quickly pinpointed.

The pediatrician's instructions started Julia off with plain, unadulterated, raw fresh fruit, grated, mashed, or whipped in a food processor, at four to five months (but never an orange before she was two or three years old). At five months, Julia moved on to simple vegetables, boiled or steamed: carrots, potatoes, zucchini, tomatoes, celery or lettuce, Swiss chard—but never spinach—followed by simple infant cereals made from rice, barley, or wheat.

At five to six months, Julia started on *pappa*, or pap, which begins as vegetable broth, moves on to a thin gruel a few weeks later, then finishes off as a thick mush. *Brodo vegetale* is the first step. One peeled carrot, one peeled potato, and one unpeeled zucchini are put into cold water and boiled until just tender. At first only the broth is offered, once a day in a bottle. Later, with only one new ingredient introduced at a time, so that potential allergic reactions can be easily tracked, other mild vegetables are added to the basic mix. As the days go by, the cooked vegetables are puréed and returned to the broth, thickening it to the point where the baby can be fed the concoction with a spoon. As more time passes, baby cereal is added; later, a teaspoon of extra-virgin olive oil; and later still, at six months, small amounts of beef, veal, turkey, rabbit, or lamb, poached or grilled, then puréed in a blender. Yogurt and mild cheeses, fish, eggs, and cow's milk follow in the next months, until the baby is considered ready for table food.

Making *brodo vegetale*, fresh every morning and fresh again each evening, kept me firmly anchored in the present, watching and helping Julia explore the world of food. I had started reading to her about the same time I was weaning her, so she was also exploring the world of sounds and pictures and words. It was a time of wonder and exploration for the two of us, and I don't think I could ever decide which I liked better, feeding her or reading to her, just as my father had read to me every night. I loved satisfying her hunger for food—which so easily translates into a hunger for love—as much as she loved having that hunger sated.

It was a magical period, both for Julia and for me, although after three or four months of making *pappa* twice a day, even my enthusiasm was beginning to flag. Making *pappa* was beginning to feel like a chore, and Julia, too, seemed to be tiring of eating the same thing each day.

Then three of John's cousins arrived in Rome for a visit. I

had made an enormous pot of *zuppa di ceci*, a thick, tasty winter soup of puréed chickpeas, tomatoes, olive oil, garlic, and a
handful of finely chopped fresh rosemary. Mary, Elizabeth, and
Vivian were seated around our table, with John at one end, me
at the other, and Julia in her high chair next to me. As I filled up
our big white soup bowls with the thick, orange-colored soup,
the rich smell of rosemary and garlic filled the room.

Julia was enjoying the hubbub, attention, and laughter as we
settled down to eat. But when I finished serving the soup, she
clearly looked deflated that she alone had been denied. I thought
about it for a moment, then went to get a smaller white soup bowl
from the cabinet, poured a scant ladleful inside, and placed the
bowl on her tray. We all dug in happily, and I offered a spoonful to
Julia. She looked a bit surprised at first swallow, but then she, too,
like the rest of us, was suddenly smiling. She took that first bowl
of adult food down in minutes, and I suddenly realized that I had
likely made my last batch of *brodo vegetale* that very morning. It was
a happy realization, utterly unlike the abrupt end of breast-feeding
a few months earlier. I called the pediatrician later in the day to
make sure Julia was truly ready to leave baby food behind, and the
doctor, listening to my description of the meal, told me she agreed
that Julia had been launched successfully. From that point on, she
ate what we ate, hungrily, with gusto and pleasure.

Julia tried, over those next days and weeks and months,
new food after new food. She ate them, smeared them, rubbed
them through her fingers and into her hair. She sang to them,

groaned for them, laughed in joy at their arrival. She developed fetishes early on, for days delighting in boiled baby onions, then switching gleefully for a week or two to tiny lumps of soft, ripe mango.

After that we experimented with a taste of mild, fresh *stracchino* cheese, Greek yogurt, a cut-up peach, a slice of ripe avocado, pear juice, veal meatballs, nectarine slices, a few lumps of butternut squash, glazed carrot sticks, fresh-squeezed tangerine juice, a whole wheat cracker, polenta with Parmigiano and tomato sauce, Swiss chard, a slice of fresh persimmon, an asparagus spear, risotto. Julia loved *frutti di bosco*—blueberries, raspberries, wild strawberries, and red and black currants served in season at Roman restaurants; grilled sea bass drizzled with olive oil and lemon juice; pasta of any size or shape, with zucchini-garlic sauce, with various tomato sauces, with meaty, brown *ragù alla bolognese*, even with one of our most strongly flavored family favorites, a thick green pasta sauce made with broccoli, garlic, parsley, and anchovy. But to this day Julia's favorite dish of all remains *spaghetti alle vongole*, that simple pasta prepared with baby clams in the shell, olive oil, white wine, plenty of finely sliced garlic, a handful of chopped parsley, and a hint of hot red pepper.

Julia's favorite snacks were Roman street food: cut-up watermelon sold in plastic cups on street corners during the hottest months of the year; roast chestnuts sold in the fall; *arancini*, balls of risotto stuffed with a square of mozzarella cheese, rolled in bread crumbs, and quickly fried. Her very favorite was *pizza bianca*, a small square of which was presented to her free of charge any and every day we stopped by our local bakery to buy the crusty, oversized loaves they baked in wood-fired ovens every day but Christmas. As she grew older, Julia learned to love the bakery's other pizzas: *pizza rossa*, which was *pizza bianca* slathered in tomato sauce; or *pizza con patate*, pizza dough baked with thinly sliced potatoes and rosemary; or *pizza bianca* covered with paper-thin slices of mortadella, the Rolls-Royce version of an open-faced baloney sandwich.

But my favorite memory of Julia's babyhood is tied up with my father's eighty-first birthday, which we celebrated the July she was two on the terrace of the lake house at Trevignano Romano. Dear friends who once lived in Rome but who had moved back to Moscow were coming to spend the night with us on their way to their annual visit to Elba.

I had planned a big fishy dinner, not the boiled lobster or the big scampi we might have eaten in Connecticut, but Mediterranean sea bream baked whole with thinly sliced potatoes, very ripe cherry tomatoes, and handfuls of freshly chopped parsley, all dribbled with good, fruity olive oil and seasoned with sea salt and freshly cracked black pepper.

Our friends told me they would take care of the first course, and they arrived in a rush of hugs and kisses with a large bottle of vodka and a plastic tubful of the best black caviar, the kind one could buy at the time only in Moscow, and with the right connections. While Julia played happily with their two girls, Celestine and I toasted slabs of rustic Italian bread, buttered it lightly, then slathered the toast with caviar. We piled those slices of toast on a huge, hot platter and set it on the long wooden table that sat near the giant wisteria vines overlooking the lake.

The adults drank icy vodka, the children drank chilled apple juice, and we all laughed and talked and toasted my father's health as the sun slowly started to sink behind the house. We drank more vodka and began nibbling the warm, crunchy toast with caviar. I had eaten caviar of that quality only once in my life, more than a decade earlier, while visiting Moscow at New Year's. For my father, it was a first, and none of us, children included, seemed to be able to get enough of it. I quickly made more toast and refilled the platter.

Julia, sitting in her jump seat and facing her grandfather at the far end of the table, watched our friends' girls, about five and eight, spread caviar on their last bit of toast. She had already eaten two enormous slabs, barely coming up for air. She looked up from her empty plate and asked, during a momentary lull in the conversation, "Mama, more bread and black jam?"

All of us burst into laughter. I was thrilled to see that at the age of two she had already learned how to celebrate the life we are given, around a table, with good food, close friends, and family.

Epilogue

Nearly a year after Julia's birth, John had long mastered his fears about restarting fatherhood, and the two of them would giggle happily on the floor together whenever John was at home. Julia delighted more than anything in the antics of "Little Man," an imaginary figure whose two legs were John's index and middle finger. Little Man got into trouble constantly, jumping onto plates, bouncing onto people's heads, falling into teacups and coffeepots, and Julia loved him most when his antics got completely out of hand and he had to be punished, forced repeatedly to sit on the edge of the dining room table, forbidden to make a peep.

Late in 1999, more than six years after we had returned to Rome, we moved to Paris. To move from southern Europe to northern Europe when its summer light is dying and the cool, pewter gray of winter is at hand was perhaps not the best idea for a family that had unknowingly become extremely attached—physically and psychologically—to Rome's glorious and comforting southern light. Even Julia, who was at first excited at the thought of moving to the city of Madeline and "twelve little girls in two straight lines," was rattled by our transfer. Shortly after we moved, she began balking at getting out of bed in the morning, no longer jumped into her clothes once she did get up, and cried whenever we left the apartment.

John, without psychiatric help for the first time in seven years, was happy to plunge into his new Paris assignment. He was happy to have left Italy, happy to be back in a more stimulating intellectual environment, happy to be brushing up on his French. The only things he, like Julia, seemed to miss were the light and warmth of Rome. The three of us, in fact, were all shocked by Paris's dirtiest little secret: that the weather in Paris is generally just a tad better than London's, that the light of the City of Light is for many months of the year largely of the electric variety. I responded to the change in air and light by developing a three-year-long attack of chronic sinusitis that no amount of Western medicines could fight. It was not until, in despair, I consulted a Vietnamese acupuncturist and homeopathic doctor whose first treatment let me breathe normally again that I found I was slowly being taken in by Paris's considerable charms.

And then, by the time I was beginning to feel at home in France, in the fall of 2002, John began to flag. A routine prostate operation went off without a medical hitch but triggered flashbacks to his shooting and everything that followed. Over the course of the following year, despite a resumption of talk therapy, he slid, slowly at first, and then faster and faster, down the long, familiar slope of depression. Ultimately, after trying the new antidepression drugs on the market, to no avail, he agreed to our doctors' urging of hospitalization and electroconvulsive therapy, a modern version of the treatment that had cured him for thirty years after he left the monastery. It was a year from diagnosis to recovery this time, but the experience was remarkably different because we knew what we were dealing with, and all of us—me included—responded much more aggressively.

Throughout the period of his slide, we followed the doctors' advice and tried to keep our home life as unchanged as possible. Night after night, I would cook one of John's favorite comfort foods for supper—spaghetti with tomato, olive oil, garlic, and a handful of basil, or a *risotto alla milanese* yellow with saffron, butter, and Parmigiano; sautéed veal scallops finished off with a touch of white wine and sage; a platter of tiny green beans or a green salad made of baby field greens. While I was throwing the meal together, for few of our favorite dishes took much time to cook, John and Julia would set the table together, correcting each other if either of them misplaced the silverware or glasses. Once the table was set, John usually disappeared into our bedroom or into his corner chair in the living room to sleep or pretend to sleep, to try his best not to cry, to at least close his eyes and mind to the world until the food was ready.

But once he heard my usual summons, "A tavola," no matter how bad he felt, he knew he was expected to pull himself together and join Julia and me at the table, then eat, hungry or not, and at least listen to the conversation if not take part in it. During the meal Julia would tell us stories from the schoolyard: which second-graders were demanding daily tributes; who hadn't done their homework; who had bled; who had cried; who had been mean or a comfort. Her stories and enthusiasms, like the simple meals I prepared, were a lifeline for each of us, keeping us afloat on those evenings when none of us could see any quick way—or any way at all—out of our latest situation.

John was hospitalized for nearly five weeks, but at his insistence, the doctors allowed him to spend weekends at home, a dispensation that made him feel less ill and that allowed him to see Julia regularly, as children were not allowed to visit the psychiatric hospital just north of Paris where he was being treated. He received eight rounds of electroconvulsive therapy during his stay and was remarkably less depressed upon his release, although all of us were shaken by the loss of a portion of his short-term memory, basically everything that had happened in the three to four months before his hospitalization. Despite that memory loss, within three months he felt well enough to try returning to work part-time.

Julia, who was six at the Christmas when John's depression descended again, was flummoxed by the change in her father, the smiling, cheerful daddy who would play with her endlessly when he got home from work. She seemed fairly fine during the course of the day, going off to school, playing with her friends. But the edges of the day were too much for her. Soon after John became ill, Julia began waking up sobbing each morning. But once she was up and dressed, once she had eaten, we would walk off to school happily, just as each afternoon we would walk home together in similar high spirits. Only as she climbed into bed would her mood swing around again, and she would lie there fretting, weeping, unable to fall asleep for hours. Julia had always had the gift of falling off to sleep in a matter of moments, without problems; now she was nervous, frightened, afraid of the dark, demanding to sleep with a light on, demanding that I read to her until she was so exhausted that she would practically pass out.

The responsibility of caring for Julia pushed me to act much faster for John's recovery than I would have had John's illness been affecting only him and me. Frightened by Julia's reactions to John's depression and understanding more and more that all of us were suffering from it, I sought help for both Julia and me early in his illness. It was an easy decision, for the one thing I knew more than anything was that I did not want my daughter growing up the way I had, knowing somehow that something was very wrong with one of her parents, but completely ignorant of what that something was. Our family doctor suggested a colleague in the neighborhood whom he described as excellent at family therapy. It was she who very quickly helped me find the right words to explain to Julia in a manner that a just-turned-seven-year-old could understand.

Your daddy, I would tell her, sitting next to her on her bed, is sick. He has a sickness called depression. Depression is a sickness that makes you feel very, very sad, even though you have nothing to be sad about. It is not your fault that he has depression. It is not my fault that he has depression. It is not his fault that he has depression. It is just a sickness that he has and he is doing everything he can to get better. He is going to two or three doctors. He will go to the hospital if he needs to. He is taking medicines that the doctors prescribe. The only thing we can do to help him get better is have fun ourselves. We cannot become sad, too. Because if Daddy sees us having fun, he will start to remember that he used to have fun, too. And once he remembers that, then the depression will start to go away. But it will take a long time, so we have to be patient. And then one day he will not be lying in bed in the dark any longer, will not be crying in his chair in the living room. He will be back being the daddy you remember.

The night I first told Julia this story, she fell asleep instantly, after nearly four months of insomnia. It was a story I had to tell and retell incessantly, however, for a seven-year-old needs repeated reassurance. Whenever Julia began experiencing sleep problems, I would sit her down before bed and talk her through the entire explanation again.

Two years later, when her father was already long back to work and very much better, Julia began experiencing sleep problems once again. I told her that she had to try to figure out what was troubling her and why. I thought Julia's insomnia was the result of a recent suicide in the family of a classmate, but my doctor and I felt that Julia would be helped most if she could figure that out for herself. It took her a few months, from spring until the night before John was due to start his summer vacation. Julia, nine at the time, came to me that night to explain what she thought had been troubling her.

"Daddy's got depression," Julia said quietly. "Does that mean I will have depression?" For the first time in my life I found I was nearly thankful that my mother had suffered from depression, for I could tell her honestly, and I did, that just because Daddy has depression does not mean that she would, too. I know that for sure, I told her, because my mother had depression and I do not.

Julia then spoke about her school friend Anna, whose aunt committed suicide on New Year's Eve. "Anna's aunt had depression and killed herself," Julia said. "Does that mean Daddy is going to kill himself, too?" Anna's aunt, I told her, had a different kind of depression, one that is harder to cure. Anna's aunt, I told her, tried to get better or pretended to try to get better, but deep down she was still getting worse. Daddy's treatment really and truly did make him feel better. And if Daddy's depression comes back or gets worse, we will bring him right back to the hospital until they make him well again. I cannot tell you for sure that Daddy will never kill himself. But I know he will try his best not to do it. And I think Daddy and you and I have learned all sorts of ways to keep him from ever feeling that bad.

My nine-year-old with the greeny gold eyes looked at me, and it was clear she was wishing that I could have answered with the same degree of certitude that I answered her first question. Still, she accepted my answer, then lobbed me the ball for the third time, with an observation that still breaks my heart at the same time that it sets me free.

"Mama," Julia said, "when Daddy got depression I felt like my real daddy went away and that a fake daddy came and took his place. It looks like Daddy but it's not really Daddy." At this, I felt tears suddenly stinging my eyes, for my nine-year-old, with her fine, wise eyes, had given me the most cogent personal description of depression that I have ever heard.

"You're right, Jules," I told her. "Depression does take away the person we know. But it doesn't necessarily take them away forever." And somehow, looking at her and taking her hands in mine, I felt that with the intimate knowledge of depression that she had deep in her soul, she had a most excellent chance of escaping the same illness that had so devastated her father's and grandmother's lives, and so changed our own.

These days we own a small stone farmhouse, a low-slung, tile-roofed place half hidden by climbing roses and grape and Virginia creeper for most of the year. Its two-foot-thick walls make it feel safe and strong and comforting, and it has enough beds tucked into odd corners that we can almost always sleep the family and friends who journey to join us there. We bought it with the idea that it might, over time, become our own Trevignano, a safe haven for us all, even if it lies deep in the center of France on a gentle rise overlooking a lazy, willow-lined river, and not in the center of Italy, on a steep hillside overlooking a crystalline lake lined by umbrella pines.

We head to the house whenever we feel the need to flee the big city, whenever I need to feel thoroughly at home. The first time I saw our house it was a cold, late-October day, and when I pushed open the door to step inside I felt the same rush of recognition I experienced the day I first saw my old house in Dallas, the sense that I was home. The same thing happened in Dallas: that white clapboard wreck of a house—whose sturdy front door, outlined by a narrow surround of white wood and tiny windowpanes—entered my heart precisely because it reminded me of old New England houses that I missed seeing in Texas.

I have only felt more at home in our farmhouse the longer we are there; the house subconsciously evokes happy memories of

all the places I have lived. I felt at home when I discovered that
fig trees and acanthus—personal icons of our life in Rome—
grew in our gently sloping meadow. I felt at home when I learned
that an ancient Roman villa lies buried on the edge of our town,
with ancient Roman artifacts occasionally popping to the surface during plowing season.

But it is not just memories of Italy that the house reawakens.
The nightly racket of frogs that croak in the quiet river at the
bottom of our meadow somehow reminds me of the mournful
wail of the foghorn in the stone lighthouse off Penfield Reef, to
which I used to love to sail in my early teens. I take comfort in
the flocks of herons, egrets, and cranes, like the geese and gulls
I used to see out our living room window in Connecticut, who
take refuge in our quiet corner of France. I feel more at home
each time Julia finds yet another fossilized seashell or ammonite
embedded in our meadow's rocky soil. When we bought the
place, we had no idea that it was once at the bottom of a vast,
prehistoric sea.

The house lies in a nature reserve, Le Parc Naturel Régional
de la Brenne, a protected wilderness of forest, moor, lake, pond,
and river punctuated by small stone villages and tiny farm
hamlets, situated two hours east of the Atlantic. Built in the
mid–eighteenth century, the house sits near the perimeter walls
of a former Benedictine priory that was broken up during the
French Revolution. It is a deep comfort for me to be able to
pray in the monastery's tiny chapel, which had been filled to its

roof with sand and stone for generations, only rediscovered last century by the forebears of the family that lives there today. I often slip into the chapel to collect myself, sometimes to pray that depression never upends us all again. But it is my ultimate comfort to know that if or when it does, we have the doctors and the methods at hand to try fighting it off another time. Violence, blood, depression, and death are, I know now, part of life. Today I recognize them, respect them, fight them, and try as much as I can to keep them at bay, but I no longer pretend that they are not as much a part of life as birth or joy or love or the laughter, comfort, and strength that grow out of a simple meal shared with family or close friends.

Soon after we bought the house, we planted an herb garden, sheltered by the tall stone walls that surround our backyard. It fast became overgrown, for like Ann and Joseph's herbs in Trevignano, our sage and rosemary bushes, our parsley, dill, verbena, and basil, even our cherry tomatoes, tend to grow to fairy-tale heights. Just after we bought the place, a gardener friend moving back to Boston gave me a small bay laurel that had lived on her terrace in Paris; it has finally taken root in our rock-infested soil and I think of her each time I break off a leaf or two to flavor a sauce or soup. The raspberry canes and the rhubarb we planted last year are already flourishing, but my blueberries and arugula are languishing, and my horseradish patch gave up the ghost. Even so, I can already picture the quince tree and another fig that we hope to plant in the meadow early next year. We are a tad too far north for persimmons, but I may plant one anyway, for memory's sake.

When I left Dallas at age thirty-one, I thought of myself as a reporter on temporary assignment abroad. I pointedly held on to the house I had restored in Dallas, unwilling to let it go, unwilling to give up my iris-filled backyard or the waist-high basil and thickets of morning glories that covered my front yard, unwilling for years to give up a home of my own even if, outside its four walls, I had never felt much at home in Texas.

I certainly did not think of myself as an emigrant when I left, although it seems that is what I have unwittingly become as the years have passed. Unlike my grandparents, who decided to emigrate, I slipped into emigrant status without really knowing that that was what I had decided to do. Perhaps the difference is that I left the country of my birth not because I needed or wanted more to eat, but because I hungered to know both the good and the bad things that my grandparents and great-grandparents had left behind.

I am nearing sixty now, with a daughter soon to enter her teens and a husband closing in on seventy, so I have two tall, long-limbed reasons other than my small, short-limbed self for getting good meals on the table two or three times a day. We still arrange our lives to be together at mealtimes, and while I do most of the cooking, John and Julia increasingly pitch in, too. John has always loved making his family's special dishes, and every Christmas he and Julia make his mother's family ravioli—

hand-rolled pasta dough filled with meat, spinach, eggs, bread crumbs, and Parmigiano. The leftover stuffing goes into a veal breast or chicken for another meal, and the kitchen floor and counters and shelves get thoroughly covered in flour and dough bits, just as they are meant to during a family pasta-making session. They purposely make far too many ravioli for a single meal so that Peter and Anna, and now Anna's Benjamin, will get their share when they arrive for their holiday visit around New Year's. Soon now we'll all have a new reason to keep cooking, for Anna and Benjamin are expecting a baby boy in a few months, about the time the strawberries will be bearing fruit down at the country house. Julia's not-so-old portable crib is already there waiting for its next occupant, whose face we are longing to see.

Already we can't wait until August, when we hope the three of them will be spending a part of the baby's first summer with us at the house. The wild blackberries will be ripe then, and Julia is making plans to pick masses of them, as she has for the last few years. Last summer she turned into the family fruit-salad maker, happy to be cutting up peaches, pears, bananas, melon, and adding raspberries from our garden and blackberries from the bramble bushes that line the hedgerows in the fields nearby. Already John and I are thinking about watching Anna's baby grow and learn to enjoy his meals the way Julia did just a few years ago.

All of us cook, I think, in part to feed our daily hunger, but just as important, and perhaps more so, we cook and eat to feed our spirits, to keep us all in the same orbit of life. As the generations turn, as our family expands, the table and its simple pleasures—never just the food, but the food and the talk, the food and the laughter, the food and the tears, the jokes, the memories, the hopes—still hold us in place, well anchored in a safe harbor. There may very well be another depression or endless other troubles, big or small, lying in wait for us, but rather than freezing in fear about what may come, we try our best to live and enjoy the lives we've been served forth.

Like my mother's mother, Jennie, I like collecting recipes from neighbors and friends wherever I have landed. I'm happiest today when my French friends teach me recipes from their families, and I teach them recipes from mine. Pascale, whose good English helped her ignore my lack of French when we first arrived in Paris, taught me to simmer garden rhubarb with a sprig or two of fresh rosemary as well as the usual sugar, a sublime addition I never would have thought to try. Our country neighbor, Jacqueline, who watches over our place when we are in Paris, brings us just-picked white asparagus from our farmer neighbors or genuine homegrown tomatoes that taste like those my father's parents used to grow. I love Jacqueline's scrambled eggs with sorrel and tomato sauce—a dish her own mother used to make—as much as she looks forward to my grandmother Jennie's sour cream coffee cake with walnuts and cinnamon.

I know that one of these days, if I live long enough to enter the world of the truly elderly, I am likely to start losing my abiding interest in food. It happened to Jennie, when she started to have those tiny strokes that no one noticed until my grandfather complained that she could no longer remember how to cook. I saw it with my mother, who in her late sixties and early seventies was worn down by the relentlessness of putting three square meals on a family table every day. Often when I would call her from England or Spain or Italy or Poland or Germany she would confess that she never knew what to cook anymore. Faced with a dinner party, which she was both eager and loath to host, she would ask me, long distance, to devise a menu. Menu in hand, she could proceed, knowing my father would help her cook. But she had lost the ability, and the *wool-eee*, to devise the plan. I saw it with my mother's sister, too. Auntie, she of the chocolate cakes, gave up cooking more than a decade before she died. Luckily Uncle Joe liked to cook, and simply took up the slack.

And I see it now with my father, still living on his own at ninety. He moves at a crawl these days, and the three meals he used to eat daily have shrunk to two. He cannot manage to make himself three meals a day any longer, unless one of them is a snack of yogurt and fruit. But while age has forced him to buy more prepared foods rather than cook everything from scratch, he still gives the occasional dinner party to very close, extremely patient friends, who are willing to wait (and wait and wait) while he painstakingly prepares an asparagus risotto, a pasta with broccoli sauce, or pork filets sautéed with leeks. My father, unlike many widowers or divorcés who have lost their spouse, never lost the friends he had when my mother was alive, because he continued to invite those same couples to dinner after her death. They in turn continued inviting him as well.

But I could see this year, during his annual winter-long stay, that he was more tired and quiet than he had been in years past. Instead of bustling into the kitchen late each morning to prepare a plentiful breakfast, as he had always done since my mother's death, he seemed relieved and thankful when I would prepare his breakfast for him, or at least help him get it ready.

Years ago I sent my father a poem that I knew he would love, even though poetry as a whole tended to scare him off. It was written by John's cousin, another John Tagliabue, a poet and longtime professor at Bates College in Maine. The first time I read Cousin John's poem about polenta, I knew I had married not only the right man but into the right family. I knew my father would recognize it, too. For a long time, a copy of "A Pure Desire on a Gloomy Drab Day" decorated my father's fridge, which chuffs noisily these days but still manages to keep his perishables cold:

O Polenta—
I want something like you
    on a foggy day—
here it is gray vague cloudy
    dreary Maine
getting cold November and I want
    something

like a yellow saint, bright, something
　to stand me
in good stead—like my grandparents'
　cooking for me,
a very bright yellow warm supper, a
　bowl like a
mother's breast to hold; yes, I want
　to be
nourished and very happy like
　a loved child—
O Santa Polenta, I am about
　to lift the
spoon and eat and be saved!

Just as I see my father's lifelong passion for food starting to slip away as he begins to struggle to get food on his table, I can see the signs of this same sea change lurking within me. Already I can sense that I will not always be eager to whip up a quick pasta sauce, sauté a bit of veal and herbs, throw together a quick salad for our nighttime meal. Luckily, I am protected from this for now by Julia, who at twelve still needs years of good food on which to grow. But once she is off on her own, I can see that the soup suppers or the yogurt-and-fruit suppers that John and I often have when she is away for an evening are very likely to propagate like weeds in an untended field.

If I manage to produce that soup myself, and serve it steaming, in big, deep bowls, with silverware and napkins neatly placed on a not overly stained tablecloth, then I know I will not yet be in my final decline. If I serve the yogurt in my mother's best glass cups, and peel and cut up the fruit to go with it, I will know that I am still hanging on. But when I start to dream of the food being placed before me, hot, steaming, and prepared by somebody else—or worse yet, when I stop dreaming of food at all—I will know that I have crossed a boundary that means I am on my way out of this world and into the next.

It is not something I look forward to. And I know it is something I will fight, just as my father is fighting it now, just as Jennie and Auntie and my mother fought it toward the end of their own lives. So tonight and all the other nights when I may be tired, without appetite, or simply not in the mood to produce even a simple meal, I shall will myself to do it anyway. I will root around the bottom of our refrigerator, check the vegetables stored on our balcony, open our tiny pantry, and find something to restore my energy and my mood.

John and Julia will set the table and I will fly about the kitchen, chopping a few garlic cloves and a handful of fragrant flat-leaf parsley. If I am lucky, I may find a package of De Cecco spaghetti in the pantry, and a bit of frozen chicken broth that I made a few weeks ago. I may find a can of sweet New England clams that my father has carried across the Atlantic for just such emergency meals. I know there is always a bottle of good, green-gold olive oil on the shelf near the stove, and a bottle of dry vermouth in the old cabinet I bought in Rome.

Tonight I will set a huge kettle of water on our tiny stove's biggest burner. By the time the water reaches a rolling boil, I will have sautéed the chopped garlic and a tiny, hot *peperoncino rosso* in a few spoonfuls of olive oil until the garlic just starts to sizzle. I will have added the vermouth and clam broth and chicken broth to the pan, then boiled it down until it has reduced by half. I will cook the spaghetti in the roiling, salted water for just under eight minutes, then heat the clams themselves for a minute or less to keep them tender and juicy. I will drain the pasta the moment it is done and tip it into a well-heated serving bowl with a tablespoon of soft butter. I will add the clams and their sauce and, finally, a handful of chopped parsley.

I will rush the bowl to the dining room and then John and Julia and I, suddenly hungry from the sweetly pungent smell of garlic and clam broth coming from the kitchen, will sit down to eat. The three of us will be quiet for a moment or two as we twirl our spaghetti into the first neat forkfuls that we lift to our mouths. We will chew that first bite hungrily and perhaps, if I have hit all the measurements right, give a tiny sigh of delight. Then, already heartened, we will start to talk and laugh and eat in earnest, keeping the feast that we are meant to keep, the feast that is our life.

Acknowledgments

This book had many midwives, both medical and literary. Profound thanks to: Harold Bourne, Flavia Donati, Veronique Durouchoux, Jacques Pieri, Henri-Paul Denis, Francis Slattery, Marianne Goldberger, Gary Lefer, Joan Prudick, Joshua Twersky, Krystyna Piotrowska, the late Petru Radulescu, Joseph Lelyveld, and to my father, brother, and late mother—in various ways, healers all.

On the literary front, heartfelt thanks to: Francis X. Clines and Esther Fein, whose telex presence from Moscow to Munich helped launch this book years before I knew I had started writing it; the late Louis Inturrisi, who was there from the beginning; Katie Hafner, Cheryl Bentsen, John Marks, Debra Immergut, and the late Marilyn Koch, who soon joined in; and Jean Frere,

Cathy Booth Thomas, Karen Wolman, Pat Remick, and Pauline Choi, who helped immeasurably near the finish. Very special thanks to Barbara Grossman, who counseled me not to write a cookbook, and to Sarah McGrath, who has an uncannily fine eye for addition and subtraction. Most important, deepest thanks to Charlotte Sheedy, whose chance acquaintance late in the process gave me the reason to pick up where I had left off.